DON'T LOOK AT THE CAMERA

THE CAMERA

The inside story of making television
at Britain's smallest ITV station

Ian Fisher

The right of Ian Fisher to be identified as author of this work
has been asserted in accordance with Sections 77 and 78 of the
Copyright, Designs and Patents Act 1988

© Ian Fisher MMXVII
First Published 2017 in the United Kingdom by Creative Imagineers Ltd.
v. 1.31
ISBN 978-1-99-981370-3

books.creativeimagineers.co.uk

CONTENTS

PREFACE

The instruction *Don't Look at the Camera* is often used in television production. It's an attempt to make a scene appear normal, usually when everyone in shot is acutely aware that they're about to be filmed, and that things they've done instinctively for as long as they can remember suddenly become awkward. A television camera seems to have that effect on people. But the phrase must be used with care. One cameraman I worked with would shout it out just as he was about to start filming. I noticed that it caused nearly everyone around to immediately look at the lens with an expression of fear on their face. His approach did little to calm a situation that many found stressful.

I tried hard to empathise with the people I put in front of the camera. Occasionally they'd be seasoned performers, but mostly they'd be appearing for the first time, and what was a run-of-the-mill part of my job could be a terrifying experience for them. So I tried to be gentle. It didn't always work.

In normal conversation we tend to make encouraging noises to reassure the speaker that we're paying attention to them or understanding what they're telling us. This motivation can be as simple as grunting or saying *Yes*. But a television audience doesn't want to hear these noises off. The viewer wants to concentrate on what the interviewee is telling them without distraction. So those of us who stand behind a camera and ask the questions develop a non-verbal method of achieving the same result. Often this involves nodding, and I've always thought it was an effective way of communicating encouragement. Until, that is, I met one particularly nervous man who constantly lost the thread of his explanation. By take six I was getting desperate, and I suppose my nodding was telegraphing that emotion, becoming more and more animated. Half way through an answer he stopped again, and my heart sank. But I couldn't help laughing at his admonition. "You're really putting me off," he said. "Can you stop nodding so much?"

There was an occasion when I was at a fire station in the Scottish Borders. I had completed the interviews, but needed some pictures to go with them. What could be better than having the fire engine drive in with its blue beacons flashing and the two-tone horn blaring? Everyone thought it was an excellent idea. So we set up the camera, and as the fire crew were about to carry out their manoeuvre I foolishly thought I should lighten any tension there may have been. I called across to them. "What mustn't you do?" They thought for a moment. "Look at the camera?" came the response. "No," I said with a smile. "Don't crash into the crew vehicle!" They laughed, and set off. A minute or so later the fire engine reappeared, an impressive sight and sound. It roared into the station yard and screeched to a halt, after which the driver very carefully, and equally forcefully, reversed into our crew vehicle.

I learned a lot from that. However hard you plan, however much you rehearse or prepare for what you want to do, life will always throw you a curveball. To use the phrase of former US Secretary of Defense Donald Rumsfeld, what you need to be very wary of are the unknown unknowns. Being prepared to deal with them is key.

In setting out to write this book I certainly had in mind that it should be an explanation of some of these unknown unknowns that have occurred around me during three decades of making television. I don't know whether I attract oddness to me, or whether I'm more observant than most at noticing it, but it has to be one or the other. Whenever I go filming, notable things happen. Often they make me laugh. Occasionally, they trouble me greatly. And almost always, in some small way, they change the person I am.

I would regularly go filming for weeks at a time, meeting people I invariably found interesting. I've spent time in the company of individuals who invented the microprocessor, masterminded the hydrogen bomb, fell asleep when they laughed, threatened me with a shotgun or set fire to their sports jacket while I was interviewing them. From each I brought something away which enriched my life, and these pages will give an insight into some of the funniest, the most interesting and most tragic of those times. This volume barely scratches the surface of the tales that wait to be told, but I hope that those I've included will open your eyes to the wondrous world that television has given me access to.

In putting these experiences down on paper I've tried to follow several rules, the most important of which is to approach areas which could be regarded as controversial with a light touch. For the most part, you'll find that many of those who appear in these pages remain anonymous. In some instances this is done specifically for reasons of respect. In others I felt that nothing helpful or relevant would come from naming them. They should be regarded as bit part actors in the cinema of life.

However, there are some who deserve to be named as an acknowledgement of the key roles they played. Some were the people behind the names which appeared in the often ignored programme credits. Their importance is much greater than a brief on-screen presence suggests. Without them, my job would have been somewhere between more difficult and impossible.

My thanks are due to cameraman Eric Scott-Parker,

and his sound recordists Allan Tarn and the late Cliff Goddard. They each showed enthusiasm, skill and determination in what were often difficult or dangerous situations, putting up with demands from me which were invariably unreasonable.

The enablers were Neil Robinson and Lis Howell, who had the unenviable task of engaging in the petty political battles which infect any organisation. It was good to know they were fighting for the principles we believed in as broadcasters, constantly aware that the real judges of our work are the people who watch the programmes.

The inspiration was James Graham, variously Managing Director and Chairman of Border Television Ltd and Border Television Plc. His wide-ranging discussions at a table in the corner of the canteen lit the fire of my imagination, and encouraged me to think and act beyond artificial geographical and cognitive boundaries to make programmes and series about some of the great challenges affecting our future.

Nearly three decades after those coffee table discussions began, we sat in a different venue and I drank far more caffeine than is good for me, surrounded by an eclectic mix of tourists exploring the nearby Hadrian's Wall, and locals who had discovered a place to be seen. This book was nearing completion, and James had been kind enough to cast his critical eye over it to offer some guidance. As we spoke, it became apparent to me that there was an intrinsic misunderstanding of our relative positions back then. He spent his time running the company, having returned to his native county from a high level post alongside the BBC's Director General, the act of doing so having saved Border Television from closure with just 48 hours to spare. In turning the company around at a time when it faced threats on a seemingly daily basis, he sought to change its profile, casting off its previous programme-making reputation by concentrating on areas of meaningful excellence. One such was science and technology, which was where I came in.

As those around us discussed the physical challenges that lay ahead for them walking the Roman Wall, we spoke of the more esoteric thinking which had realised those ambitions. In the context of our setting, we had altered the perspective of the company, eschewing the practicalities of an 84 mile hike to gain an understanding of the reasons for the Wall's existence, here at the very edge of a hugely powerful empire.

James explained that he felt I had recognised his desire to raise our game with programmes taking a world view of events and discoveries which touched the region we served. I was forced to confess I could claim no such prescience in my actions, at least not overtly. I have long admired his computer-like analysis of situations, as he plans the necessary moves to achieve his goals with an infinite attention to detail. In comparison, I have a much more intuitive approach, feeling my way through the undergrowth of decision making until a path appears.

As the conversation progressed it was clear that our thinking had been parallel rather than combined. It had not been a planned campaign as he believed. Instead, the process which had moved us from a regional broadcaster, obsessed by its artificial borders and derided by its larger and richer cousins, to a world player held up by the regulator as an example to those very critics of what they should be aspiring to achieve, had come about through a perfect storm. He had removed the shackles which constrained me, allowing an expansion of my thinking in a way that he alone fully understood. And this was why a programme maker from Britain's smallest ITV company would come to sit in the company of some 20th century greats; people who had changed the world like Dr Edward Teller, Gordon Moore and Eric Schmidt.

There's one remaining person whose role in this transformation should be acknowledged. I had always narrated my own programmes, but only because of my roots in news journalism. I was well aware of the inadequacies of my voice, and as time went on felt the need to apply a higher quality veneer to my productions. It came in the form of the late Tim Pigott-Smith. He was a giant of a man, both in stature and ability. As a stage and screen actor he was developing an enviable reputation, but it was his narration work which brought him to my attention. Tim's rich and melodious tones adorned many documentaries, and I knew he would provide an extra authority to my work.

Many were surprised that I was able to persuade him to work with me. The budgets I had available were laughable by his standards, yet he must have seen what I was trying to achieve, and became an enthusastic supporter over the years. I would sit in the control room at Wild Tracks, our preferred audio studio in Soho, and listen in awe as a metamorphosis took place. With a consummate ease, he demonstrated the imperfections of my own guide track laid down in the edit suite, replacing it with a gifted performance, deceptive in its apparent simplicity, which cast light and shade on the carefully crafted script. They were emotional episodes which gave the programmes life.

John Myers, who went from local radio presenter to broadcasting impresario, told me of a meeting one evening with the company's financial director, the late Peter Brownlow. While they worked their way through the agenda, Peter's television was on in the corner of his office. At first no more than a slight background distraction, it slowly drew a growing level of attention until, eventually, the meeting was abandoned as the two of them became mesmerised by the programme on air. John told me of his astonishment when a familiar blue caption appeared at the end, marking it as a Border Television production. The programme was *Are we Alone...?*, from my science and technology series *Innovators*, which dealt with the search for extraterrestrial intelligence. He told me how amazed he had been by the sight of that caption.

It was exactly the reaction James Graham and I were seeking, and was a clear sign that we had achieved our goals. We would go on to win approval for my programmes from other sources such as the New York Film and Television Festival, the Royal Television Society and BAFTA, each underpinning our determination to continue, no matter how overwhelming the task might appear.

The Chinese General, Sun Tzu, wrote in *The Art of War*, *If you wait by the river bank long enough, the bodies of your enemies will float by*. His exhortation to embrace patience is a difficult concept for me. I've always been in a hurry to get places. But if I've learned anything over the years, it's been to try my best to enjoy the journey. It's my hope that *Don't Look at the Camera* provides evidence that I succeeded.

ARM OF A PRINCESS

If you look at me you'll see a pretty unremarkable person. I'm not overtly tall, athletic or handsome. But, beneath this rather ordinary façade there lies a surprising secret. I have an extraordinary arm. I have to confess, such is the fogging effect of the passage of time, that I have difficulty remembering which of my arms is so special, but I think it's probably the right one. What I'm about to reveal has, until now, been known only to a relatively small number of people, although those who are aware may not necessarily have been particularly impressed. But for me, the role my arm has played is a source of satisfaction and pride. It has done what few, if any, other arms can claim to have achieved. It has impersonated Princess Anne.

The event took place in the 1980s, that decade when big hair and shoulder pads were de rigueur, George Michael was in the charts but hadn't yet been to Snappy Snaps, and Margaret Thatcher had a long term lease on 10 Downing Street. I had come to work as a television reporter and presenter at Britain's smallest ITV station and was slowly learning how to respond to the myriad of banana skins life dropped in my path as I tried to capture microscopic parts of history and interpret their meaning for the nightly audience. I was quickly compiling a list of my favourite and not-so-favourite types of story. Each demanded its own unique approach and response, but once I had tackled a few from a particular category the banana skins could be anticipated and, with a combination of luck and skill, avoided. Or at least that's what I hoped.

The easiest stories to do were those which afforded total control. I'd turn up with a film crew at someone's house and automatically take charge of the situation. It was astonishing how compliant people become when faced with a television camera, so I would work out how to turn the tale they had to tell into something which would make sense on the small screen and they'd pretty much go along with what I asked them to do. Having been brought up in the BBC with its strict editorial policies, I tried to exercise this control in what I hoped was a fair and measured manner. And in general I think I was pretty successful.

At the opposite end of the spectrum were the stories over which I had absolutely no control, where I was simply an observer of events. One of my technical colleagues thought he understood the difference well. This was, he said, hard news, because it was hard to get. It has been described as a record of the misfortunes of others, and I've often been uncomfortable with the side of life it showed me.

One pleasant morning I was on my way to film in the Scottish Borders, north of Hawick. Somewhere past the community of Denholm, the road lies in wait for the unwary traveller. It's a small country road, single carriageway, meandering through a beautiful landscape of rolling hills and fertile farmland. But there's a section worthy of the greatest of Formula One race track designers, laid out to trap even the most skilful of drivers. You're bowling along, enjoying the sunshine and the view, lost in thought about what you're going to have for supper that night or your forthcoming holiday somewhere warm, unaware of Lorelei ahead enticing you onto the rocks. The road curves gently, encouraging a balanced response as you position the vehicle carefully to maximise the conservation of energy and minimise the loss of speed. Each curve reverses the direction of motion, at first subtly, but then with a growing sense of urgency until, before you know what's happening, the demands of the highway exceed the talent of driver or adhesion of tyres. That morning, a man had set out from north-west England's industrial belt to make a delivery. Perhaps he'd never travelled this stretch of road before. Maybe he treated it with the casual familiarity of a trusted friend. But on that quiet and peaceful summer's day Fate took its hand and slapped him in the face.

When we chanced upon the scene of the accident,

the police had already arrived. We stopped, and I automatically began to form a course of action. My cameraman that morning was an unknown quantity. He was a freelance from Glasgow, and I'd never worked with him before. But he was no youngster, and seemed to know what he was doing. I sent him to get some pictures of the scene while I talked with one of the policemen, trying to construct the series of events which put driver and van where they'd ended up. Fate had been unbelievably cruel. Leaving this road nearly anywhere along its length would have resulted in little more than a journey through a fence and across a field, producing a bruised ego, a bill for repairs and a lecture from the boss. However, the crucial word is *nearly*. At the point just past the apex of the final, imperceptibly tighter turn where the van had left the road, stood a tall, mature, immovable tree which had brought progress to a swift and violent halt.

As I stood in discussion with the policeman, my back to the scene of the crash, his colleague approached from behind. With an almost apologetic diffidence he said, "Can you have a word with your cameraman. I don't think the driver's going to make it." I turned around, and was horrified by the scene. The front of the van was crushed by its impact with the tree, trapping the dying driver in his seat. Alongside him, standing on the access step to the cab, was my cameraman, filming his final moments from a foot away. For a second I couldn't believe what I saw. How could anyone behave in such a callous, uncaring way? I apologised as best

I could to the officer, before sprinting down the road to haul camera and operator out of the cab. As I gave him a lecture about boundaries and acceptable images it dawned on me that I was dealing with someone who had little or no experience of news. Looking at the world through the viewfinder of a camera is not far removed from watching the scene from the comfort of your armchair. It sanitises the events taking place before you, rendering a remoteness which removes any sense of reality. This was the first time I'd witnessed it, but would experience something similar myself on occasions in the coming years. In part, I reasoned, it was a necessary aspect of the job, allowing an objectiveness which would otherwise be clouded by emotion. I still think of that driver from time to time. His death on an otherwise pleasant morning was many lessons for me, not least of which was how fragile the existence we take for granted really is. And how unpleasant covering events over which I had no control could sometimes turn out to be.

I had a friend on the Isle of Man who worked for the Manx government. Derek was a genius at inventing ways of bringing tourists to the island. Such was his success that people were comfortable accepting the most outrageous notions of sporting occasions simply because he'd come up with a clever wheeze. During one of our trips, my regular cameraman, Eric, suffered from a bad attack of gout. For many, the affliction brings to mind elderly colonels, having indulged in a little too much Port, sitting in front of the fire with a foot supported on a chair. It's generally seen as something to have a quiet chuckle about. But anyone who's suffered from gout knows how exquisitely painful it is. Rather than retire to a comfy chair, Eric had carried on working. In an attempt to ease the pressure on his big toe joint, he had taken to wearing a carpet slipper on the affected foot, whilst the other still sported his trademark stout, brown brogue. It looked a slightly bizarre sight, but I'd become used to it. As we checked in at the airport for the flight home, the agent behind the counter noticed the footwear imbalance and asked about it. Without a pause, Eric replied, "I've been across for the Manx Hopping Championships," an obviously entirely fictitious event, though only so, perhaps, because Derek hadn't yet thought of it. I made a mental note to suggest it next time I saw him. There was no reaction of surprise at all from the other side of the counter. Feeling slightly let down by this casual acceptance, Eric smiled at her disarmingly. "I didn't win anything, unfortunately," he said. She smiled back and replied, "Never mind. There's always next year."

One of Derek's more enjoyable extravaganzas was a vintage car rally, and I was persuaded to come and film it. Most events on the island seemed to involve the consumption of copious quantities of alcohol, and a welcome party was organised one lunch time to introduce these well-heeled car owners to such Manx customs. It was here that I met Hamish Moffatt. I had learned from filming at these affairs that the most important person to make friends with was whoever had been tasked with keeping the wine glasses filled. I thought I was quite good at it, and we never went thirsty. But Moffatt made me look and feel like a rank amateur. He swept into the reception with his wife and daughter in tow, grabbed a huge silver salver of chicken legs, two bottles of champagne and some glasses, and exited to the balcony for a very pleasant lunch in the sunshine. I exchanged a look with Eric, and although we said little aloud about the man's obvious style, we both parked it away in memory for future reference and impersonation.

Hamish had brought his Type 35 Bugatti, a car worth serious amounts of money. It was absolutely beautiful, dressed in the shade of blue its heritage as an Italian racing car demanded. Despite its value, the owner was less than shy about throwing it around. At the organised time trials on the disused airfield at Jurby, he was kind enough to show me around it. The most interesting feature was the exposed prop shaft which ran through the cockpit. Hamish explained that he wore a special pair of leather shoes when he drove the car, so that the shaft had something solid to rotate against which provided protection for his foot. The programme made it to air a month or two later, and was well received, mainly because of the beautiful cars and their eccentric owners.

The people we rubbed shoulders with, including Hamish, faded to the back of my mind, but Eric and I would occasionally speak in awe of the wonderful technique we'd witnessed for the appropriation of alcohol. A lot of years passed by, until Saturday 10th August 2002, when my phone rang. It was Eric, and he told me he had just opened his copy of the Daily Telegraph to find the face of Hamish staring out at him. Sadly, the man we had admired so much had died at the age of 71. "You've got to read his obituary," Eric said. "It's amazing." So I found the article and settled down to read, learning why Hamish Moffatt would think nothing of snaffling a couple of bottles of champagne and a few chicken legs at a reception. The man had certainly been a character. He'd had a life-long love of cars and aeroplanes. The Bugatti he took to the Isle of Man was one of three he owned. He also had three vintage aircraft. At the age of 21 he decided to drive as much of the length of Africa as finances would allow, and so on 21st December 1952 he set off alone in an 11.9 hp 1923 Lagonda Tourer on an epic 12,500 mile journey, eventually making it to Cape Town. The trip was not without incident. After making an unintended 200 mile detour to cash a traveller's cheque, he cut across country to intercept his original route. Unfortunately, at one point the track he was following simply petered out, and he was forced to navigate across the desert at night using nothing more than the stars and a compass. After five or six hours he spotted a light in the distance which turned out to be the town of El Aricha in northwest Algeria. Hamish gave a lift to a young Dutchman he met outside a brothel in Columb Becher and they took turns at driving, the Dutchman managing to overturn the Lagonda twice. By the time they reached Nairobi, Hamish had repaired a grand total of 57 punctures, along with the damage from both crashes. But Africa wasn't his only driving adventure. In November 1969 he set off on an even longer trip, driving through France, Italy, Greece, Turkey, Afghanistan and India, before making the trans-continental journey across Australia. He would later write that, across the whole land mass of India, he was never out of sight of another human being.

Hamish won 200 racing trophies, and his competitiveness is shown in a famous photograph of him cornering his 1923 Bugatti T23 Brescia at the Pardon Hairpin on the Bugatti Owner's Club track near Cheltenham. The rear nearside wheel is obscured by the body of the car, but the front nearside is so far off the ground that the rear must be also. His enthusiasm for cars was mirrored by his enjoyment of aircraft. Perhaps his most memorable recorded moment took place above the car park of the Verzons Hotel in Trumpet near Hereford. He'd set off in his Currie Wot biplane with the intention of flour bombing a 1903 Mercedes Benz at a Vintage Sports Car Club meeting. Unfortunately, for whatever reason, his aim was a little imprecise that day. His friends, rather than the Mercedes-Benz, were covered in flour, while another improvised missile hit the hotel roof, and a smoke bomb set fire to the roses. The Civil Aviation Authority didn't see the funny side, and relieved him of £500. The obituary taught me that my instincts about Hamish had been right. He was someone who stood out from the crowd by a mile. And he was the first of many people I was lucky enough to spend time with who contributed something tangible, not only to my life, but to the lives of many around them.

Sometime after the vintage car rally I got another call from Derek. This time, he'd organised a pre-season football tournament, and some of the big clubs were taking part. It seemed too good an opportunity to miss, so I agreed to go and film it. It wasn't until I was sitting in the stadium just before kick-off that I realised I'd probably bitten off a little too much. I'd assumed, without really giving it much thought, that this would be a story like any other. However, it was probably only the second game of football I'd ever attended. The first had been when I was about eight years old. From my seat in the stand everything seemed so much further away than it is on television. And worse, there wasn't a commentator to tell me what was happening. This intrinsic ignorance was compounded by a severe technical limitation which was nearly my downfall. In those days we shot on film, so there would be no pictures for me to see until they emerged from the processing bath, and that was a hundred miles away across the Irish Sea in Carlisle. Ten years later, I could have reviewed a videotape and written my script to the pictures I saw, but here I was effectively blind. I quickly decided on a course of action. I opened my notebook and furiously began writing down the numbers on the shirts of players who touched the ball when it headed anywhere close to goal. The plan was that, when someone scored, I could backtrack through the numbers and pull the names from the match programme to make some sense of it for the viewer. Thankfully, as I remember, there were few goals, and my amateurish approach allowed me to write some suitable commentary that didn't seem to attract any complaints. However, the incident persuaded me to add football matches alongside road accidents to the list of stories I would try to avoid in future.

Royal visits were different. They were a gladiatorial contest, where our skills were pitted against chance. And it was rare for chance to win. It was on these occasions that I began to evolve an interesting relationship with Eric. He had a good nose for news, having spent years working as a freelance where he didn't earn if he didn't turn up stories. I learned a lot from him, and developed what American songwriter Sammy Cahn once explained to me was called *chutzpah*. The word is Hungarian, and here's no direct equivalent in English. The nearest is *cheek*. There was one Royal visit in particular which involved chutzpah in bucket loads.

Part of my reason for enjoying these Royal events was down to another participant. Oliver Prince-White was the Royals' man on the ground. He worked for the COI, the government's Central Office of Information, and was the keeper of the Royal passes. Without these vital pieces of card you couldn't get close to the action. Oliver acted as sheepdog when a Royal personage was in town, herding the press pack and ensuring, as far as was possible, that its members' behaviour didn't become too unseemly in the search for a story. He was ideal for the task, both charming and urbane, presenting the perfect image of a civil servant as he strode about, always it seemed, holding a rolled-up umbrella lest there be an unexpected inclemency of the weather. I quickly earned Oliver's trust for some reason, and he was confident enough I'd behave that he'd pretty much leave me alone. It meant that I would often get us into positions the rest of the pack couldn't get near.

Key to these events going well was my relationship with Eric. It was on endless Royal visits that I began to develop a technique which would serve us well when we covered the Isle of Man TT Races. He could only really see what the camera was focussed on, though occasionally he did have a slightly scary habit of opening his other eye and swivelling it around to observe what he was missing. Thankfully, it largely remained tightly shut. While he captured the images, I was constantly scanning around, looking for interesting shots which would help tell the story. I love people watching, and Eric's unparalleled expertise at capturing the moment was a joy to be able to direct and use. There were many little foibles in his character, each adding a further layer of interest and humour. Amongst them was an occasional propensity for dieting. I always knew when a diet was under way because, at often unexpected times of the day, a sandwich wrapped in cling film would appear from the pocket of his blue anorak. These items of clothing were standard wear for all of us road warriors. Eric's held his sandwiches and a pair of grey woollen gloves to protect his hands when temperatures were low and he needed to maintain dexterity to operate the camera. Mine contained a veritable cornucopia of items which were part of what I described as my Junior Reporter's Outfit, the sort of items you could imagine seeing advertised in The Boy's Own Magazine, complete with an explanatory diagram. Cliff, Eric's often cranky but always lovable sound recordist, was regularly disdainful of the demands of my job. "We have to carry all this equipment," he would say. "All you have to do is turn up with a pencil."

Those who politely offered to hang up my anorak when we went to film in their home would discover my needs were considerably more onerous than Cliff imagined. Whilst supposedly in charge of the crew, it always seemed to me that they regarded me as their pack horse. My anorak's capacious pockets were the ideal place to store spare camera batteries, and as technology moved forward, camera tapes and a huge mobile phone. The jacket, you'll appreciate, became very heavy. Mostly when I handed it over to be hung up, the surprising weight meant it would immediately hit the floor. In the end I decided to cut out the middle man and simply abandoned it there myself.

Eric's cling film wrap inevitably contained his standard diet fare of Marmite on white bread. I always knew the days he was struggling to maintain his reduced food intake. The sandwiches would appear as we drove down the on-ramp to the motorway, five minutes after we left the studio in the morning. The other challenging days posed a moral dilemma, or perhaps one of self-will. People we were filming with would sometimes invite us to have lunch with them. One of our favourites was a company called Cavaghan & Gray, directly across the road from the studios. They created ready-made meals and snacks for Marks & Spencer, and lunch there was always a treat. But for Eric, these invitations were akin to the Devil's Temptation. I could see the cogs whirring inside his brain as he balanced the benefits - an invariably delicious meal - against the downside - failure of the diet. I rarely remember him refusing an offer. So the meal was inhaled with gusto, and his sandwiches would later be consumed on the way home from the next job.

When Princess Anne came to Carlisle, we were assigned to cover her visit. At that time we worked as a crew of four. Aside from Cliff, Eric and me there was an electrician, his presence a throwback to the power of the unions when ITV was formed. Most of them played their part as a member of the crew, casting aside demarcation issues to help out with the more important task of just getting the job done. Some were less than helpful, preferring to spend what would become a boring day doing nothing if their primary role of providing lighting wasn't required. On this particular shoot, we were accompanied by Gordon, one of the electrical department's more colourful characters. Gordon enjoyed playing a game of one-upmanship. He would tell the most outrageous fibs. But there was a clever mixture of fact and fiction in his stories which meant that, when you finally had enough of his nonsense and challenged one of his claims, it would inevitably be over something he could prove was true. One of the less likely ones was his insistence that he got a Christmas card each year from Joseph Mengele, the infamous Doctor of Death from Auschwitz. He would regale us with tales of how he'd driven to the south of France and back over the weekend. And when Gordon had his heart attack, it was in truly glorious fashion. For some reason I can't recall, he'd decided to raise the roof of his garage by a few inches, so he climbed a set of ladders, put his shoulders against the rafters and pushed up until he could slide in a brick to hold it in place. When faced with a battle between the weight of the garage roof and the strength of Gordon's heart, the roof was the undisputed victor.

There were many occasions when the humour of the moment shone through. Eric, Cliff and Gordon had gone to see a retired army general to do an interview. The reporter was a close friend of mine, Michael, who happened to come from Jersey. Gordon joined in with the small talk about the armed forces with enthusiasm, and mentioned he'd been in the army during the Second World War. The general had a sensitive nose for the story-teller, and gently asked, "So where did you serve during the war, Gordon?" Gordon was quick to reply. "I was based on Jersey," he said. Michael's head snapped round, his face a picture of puzzlement. "But Gordon," he said. "We were occupied during the war." Without pausing, even for a heartbeat, Gordon shot back a confident "That's right!" Four brains computed this information. Everyone knew this was one of Gordon's tall tales, even if the general was only just discovering them. Would anyone be brave enough to challenge the claim? In the end it was the general who spoke first. With a small smile on his lips he laid his trap. "And what were you doing there?" he enquired. Gordon gave the man a withering look. "You should know better than to ask that!" he said with a sad shake of his head. The others suppressed their own grins at the general's discovery that you had to be very sharp to get the better of Gordon.

The first part of Princess Anne's day involved a visit to Carlisle's magnificent 12th century cathedral. Renovation work was being undertaken, and the Princess Royal had come to see how it was progressing. The interior of the building was dim, and we struggled to find enough light for filming. Those 12th century architects had failed to provide convenient power sockets for our lights. So, after a while, I decided we should quit while we were ahead, and led the crew back outside into the sunshine. Since we couldn't do much more inside the building, I thought we should show the work being carried out on the roof, which had been clad in copious amounts of scaffolding. Neither Eric nor I are fond of heights, but I had a very strict rule that I would never ask anyone to do something I wasn't prepared to do myself. So the four of us set about climbing ladders to roof level. In itself, it wouldn't have been a particularly enjoyable experience, but matters were compounded by the necessity of getting the equipment up there as well. I got off somewhat lightly, reminding Cliff that I had my pencil to carry, and was able to use both hands to hang on. My legs were shaking too much to be of any particular use. Eric managed the camera, and Gordon carried the tripod, an industrial strength wooden contraption which wouldn't have looked out of place on a Hollywood film set of the 1920s. We finally reached the summit, and began to move along the scaffolding boards forming the walkway, with the ground a terrifyingly long way below. Eric went first, carrying the camera, with me behind him, my pencil thankfully safe in the pocket of my anorak. The others followed on behind. It was then that the first of the day's surprises arrived.

Surprises, by their very nature, are unexpected, and often require an immediate, instinctive response. The brain is well designed to cope with this situation. At the heart of the response lies the amygdala, which deals with the process known as fight or flight. If a threat is perceived as immediate, it initiates swift action, deciding whether to fight it or run away. Otherwise, the information is passed on to the neocortex, which takes a little extra time to carry out more complex analysis. I've worked with people who rarely allow decisions to pass beyond the amygdala. Dealing with these colleagues has always been a frustrating experience, since they are swayed by an emotional first response, rarely looking beyond this to think about wider ranging factors and interactions. This particular surprise was definitely one for the amygdala to deal with. With no warning, the scaffolding board Eric was transferring his weight to collapsed, and he and the camera immediately began a plunge to earth. It wasn't exactly fight or flight, but at least my brain recognised the situation called for quick, decisive action. While my neocortex struggled to keep up with unrolling events, I found myself grabbing the hood of Eric's anorak and arresting the descent almost before it began. I hauled him back up to my level and we continued on our way. I don't remember any great drama being made of what I've just described. We didn't stand around and worry about what might have been. We simply got on with what we had to do, and put the surprise behind us. Perhaps I should have calculated this was a sign that the day had prepared a number of shocks of varying types to test the way we'd respond. As it turned out, we met them all head-on and emerged victorious.

Filming on the roof took but a few minutes, and it was soon time to return to the safety of the ground. We reversed direction and gingerly began to inch our way back towards the ladders. Once again, I was grateful I only had my pencil to worry about. For Eric, the task of manhandling the camera downwards demanded care and attention. But for Gordon, with the heavy wooden tripod balanced on his shoulder, the prospect seemed particularly unpalatable. So instead of carrying it down the ladders, he chose the easy option and tossed it over the side. I watched with a sense of disbelief as it began its journey eighty feet to the grass below. I felt the day was beginning to slip from my control. But worse was to come, because circumstances took an unfortunate turn at this point. At about the same time as the tripod and Gordon parted company, Princess Anne emerged from the cathedral entrance just a few feet away. There was probably little chance that tripod and Royal personage were going to attempt to occupy the same piece of real estate at the same moment in time, but nevertheless even the mildest of the potential newspaper headlines filled me with dread. Yet, to my astonishment, no-one seemed to notice. The unfolding scene snapped out of its slow-motion state as the tripod head struck the ground with a dull thud, leaving a tell-tale crater at the point of impact. Despite the ferocity of the arrival, Princess Anne didn't flinch. None of the police, Special Branch or Royal Protection officers seemed to notice, and no firearms were drawn. Even the press pack missed what surely could have been the story of the day. So we waited for the Princess to walk past, pretending we were suddenly invisible, before going to retrieve the thankfully undamaged tripod from the newly designed hole in the grass. As casually as possible, we followed the rest of the travelling multitude the short distance to the Crown and Mitre hotel for lunch.

Oliver from the COI directed us downstairs to a side room where he said the press lunch had been prepared. Royal visits were carefully stage-managed, with accurate timing of events being of great importance. Providing lunch for us all was a way of ensuring that we were kept on a short leash and wouldn't cause Oliver problems when he wanted us to leave. It was also a pleasant interlude. I led the crew in through the door, and was met with the sight of a trestle table covered by a pristine white table cloth, and bearing all manner of goodies. Predominant amongst them were three large silver salvers containing a selection of sandwiches. To my disappointment, I noticed that they were all made with brown bread. I'm not a fan of brown bread, but beggars can't be choosers, or so the saying goes. The press party consisted of journalists and photographers, mainly from local papers, us and a film crew from the BBC. We knew a few of the newspaper guys, and despite the rivalry, regarded the BBC crew as friends. The room divided naturally into print and broadcast teams, with us in the minority. So in the spirit of fairness and even-handedness I picked up one of the salvers of sandwiches and headed for some tables in the corner, leaving the other two for the newspaper guys to fight over. We were joined by the BBC, and began to tuck in. I noticed that Eric was looking slightly embarrassed, and began to grin broadly when I realised the reason. While the rest of us were enjoying salmon and cucumber on brown, Eric pulled his cling film wrapped Marmite on white from his anorak pocket, and with a look on his face which attempted to claim him the moral high ground, started to eat. Within a few minutes both salver and cling film contained nothing but crumbs, and we began to talk about what lay ahead for the afternoon.

It was then that something quite extraordinary happened. A door opened - a different one from the one we'd entered through - and a crowd of uniformed and plain clothes police entered. They were led by a detective who was doing a passable impersonation, given his body language and expression, of the station hard man. Conversation ceased as police and journalists eyed each other up. The detective took in the room with the practised eye of the trained observer he undoubtedly was. In an instant he committed the scene to memory. It was a technique I knew well from a situation I could have lived without on the Isle of Man.

Each year I would travel to the island's premier sporting event, the TT races, where intrepid motor-cyclists risked their lives to thrill the crowds around the 37 mile mountain circuit, travelling at speeds approaching 200 miles an hour. Eric and I would arrive on the island early in Practice Week, and invariably at the start of the first race I would bump into the Chief Constable, Robin Oake. I knew Robin well, having gone to the headquarters of Greater Manchester Police, where he'd previously worked, to interview him when he was appointed to the job. Robin was an imposing figure of a man, standing around six feet six inches tall, and invariably looked immaculate in his dress uniform. In his right hand there was always a highly polished night stick with a silver top. This was a lethal weapon if I ever saw one. On this occasion, I was standing with the crew at the front of the vehicle we'd brought across on the ferry, discussing the plan for the race. Taking the vehicle to the island made life a bit more difficult than it would have been if we'd travelled by air, but it meant we were able to operate from a familiar workspace, have all the equipment to hand, and since it was liveried with the company logo it also provided a good bit of PR. Robin greeted me, and we all shook hands. As we spoke, I couldn't help noticing his eyes taking in everything around, constantly on the lookout for something out of the ordinary to catch his attention. I didn't have to wait long. In mid-sentence he raised his night stick and tapped it on the windscreen of our vehicle. "Your tax disc is out of date," he said. I blanched, before looking to confirm he was right. Of course he was. It had run out at the end of May, just after we had left for the island, and here we were, by now at the beginning of June. The new tax disc, presumably, was in someone's desk back in Carlisle awaiting our return. I apologised profusely and explained the circumstances, and although I seemed to appease him, for a few moments there was a frostiness in the air that signified we'd strayed away from friendship to enter the world of business. I was relieved when he didn't take any action, and on our return home, I mentioned the incident to the person who was Head of Tax Discs. I expected they would reassure me and show suitable penitence. Instead, they simply laughed. The following year Eric and I were back at the TT, standing in the sunshine on the first Saturday in June awaiting the start of the inaugural race. Once again, the Chief Constable paused to say hello. And for a second time he tapped the windscreen with his night stick. Head of Tax Discs still hadn't learned their lesson.

As the detective's eyes swept the room, they came to

rest on the salver I'd carried over to our corner. I could see a crimson tide of anger rise up his neck and colour his face. He pointed an accusing, shaking finger at Eric, the nearest person to him, and with barely controlled rage shouted, "You have eaten the police sandwiches!" It seemed Oliver had directed us to the wrong room. If the groups had been subdued before, they were now utterly silent. As my neocortex began to scrabble for a way out of this situation, the amygdala deftly stepped in. I stood up, and said in a slightly mocking tone, "You couldn't be more wrong!" The detective was shocked that someone dared to speak to him like this. There was a collective gasp from his colleagues as they waited for the next move. I held out my hand for Eric's cling film, which he produced from his anorak pocket. "If you would like to examine the evidence," I said, mimicking the defence attorney at a crucial turning point in the trial, "you'll see that the crumbs in Eric's cling film are white." His eyes took in the evidence. "Whereas the crumbs on the plates" - dramatic pause - "are brown." With a triumphant look that Perry Mason would have been proud of I struck the killer blow. "You call yourself a detective? You've picked on the only person in the room who hasn't had one of your sandwiches." I'm sure I heard a pin drop in the far corner. There was a long pause while the detective sought a response. Eventually, his body gave up waiting for his brain to catch up, and without another word he turned around and stalked out. When door closed behind the last of the group, the room exhaled a collective sigh and conversation slowly resumed. No-one said anything about the exchange.

But I got a little smile of thanks from Eric.

That wasn't the only time when our normally excellent relationship with the police went awry. It wasn't always our fault, but it was occasionally over something more serious than a few sandwiches. There were two incidents around the time of the Isle of Man TT which would fall into this category, and as with the case of the out of date tax disc, the less serious one took place over two consecutive years. Covering the TT was an enormous challenge for everyone involved. The camera operators bore a huge responsibility on their shoulders, and needed a wide-ranging set of skills for everything to come together. They also required a keen awareness of their surroundings at all times. Inevitably, with high powered bikes performing average lap speeds of more than 120 miles an hour on twisting public roads, there would be a temptation for some of the spectators who had brought their own machines to the island to try to emulate them. As a result, there were serious accidents along with the occasional death. There's a strong community spirit amongst those who travel on two wheels, and the sight of crumpled bike and rider would bring powerful emotions to the surface. It was at one such accident that a cameraman met trouble head-on.

It's easy to lose control of a machine on the mountain section, and one day Mike chanced on an incident not long after the roads had re-opened at the end of racing. He did what any news cameraman would do. He started filming the aftermath. Normally, he'd work alongside a journalist who, being the words man, would be expected to talk their way out of any trouble that came about. On this occasion he was alone, and when Mike produced his camera he was chased off by some angry and emotional bystanders. He told me what had happened when he arrived back at our hotel base, having made his escape relatively unscathed. As the tale unfolded, I realised that things could have turned very ugly, and Mike, understandably, had felt isolated and afraid. His safety was my responsibility, and I began to wonder what we could do differently to protect crew members who were working on their own. In a situation such as the one Mike had met you relied upon someone being sensible enough to calm things down, perhaps one of the group of bikers, or even someone who had a perceived level of authority. As it happened, there had been one such individual there, but he was far from helpful. The actions of a race marshal, one of the hundreds of volunteers who willingly gave up so much of their time to make the TT races happen, were not entirely clear, but as a minimum he had just stood by and watched. There may have been confusion about whether he had encouraged the crowd or simply not intervened, but his behaviour had fallen well short of what was acceptable. When Mike finished his story, I felt my own sense of anger over how he'd been victimised in this way. If nothing else, I felt the marshal in question should be spoken to and be encouraged to take a more positive approach to his responsibilities. I called a senior police officer I knew well to ask advice, and the conversation led to a visit from a couple of the local bobbies. They took details from Mike, and the word came back to us that action would be taken against the marshal to ensure he wasn't allowed to hold the same position of authority again. We were all satisfied that a clear signal had been given.

Each TT, I tried to ensure that the camera operators worked the same patch so that they knew where to find the best vantage spots and how to travel quickly and safely between them on narrow and twisty side roads. The following year we all returned to the island for another week of exciting, high octane racing, and I was surprised when Mike reported that he'd seen the marshal from the previous year's incident working back at the same spot. I put in a call to my police contact again to ask why the reassurance we'd been given had seemingly fallen by the wayside. A few days later he called me back, and explained that someone had taken it upon themselves to ignore instructions and effectively sweep the matter under the carpet. In order for the officer involved to be dealt with, Mike was asked to make a complaint. A few weeks later, two people turned up to interview Mike at our home base. I met them at reception and took them to the board room where he was waiting. I may have been over-sensitive, but throughout the process I felt there was a resentment in the room, with an inference that the officers who had come to see Mike blamed us for making trouble for one of their own. I wanted to say, "We didn't ask for this!" but it probably wouldn't have done much good. However, we didn't see the marshal again.

The other event could have been very serious, but turned out in my eyes at least, to be very funny instead. Eric and I were on the island for Practice Week. We were mounting a camera on a sidecar during two of the races, and needed to spend some time perfecting the process before we were faced with doing it for real. We attracted some criticism from another television crew who were more regularly involved in motor sport, largely I think because we'd beaten them to the punch with such an innovative approach. But we ended up having the last laugh. Our on-board camera never lost a race, and also recorded the first-ever 100 miles an hour average lap speed by a sidecar. On the Wednesday morning I took an urgent call from the newsroom. Although by then I no longer worked for news, I would be feeding them daily race coverage the following week, and they were aware that Eric and I were already on the island. A big news story had broken, and they were desperate to have it covered. Unfortunately, their local freelance cameraman was unreachable, and an associate who worked with him had an inexplicably urgent appointment with a hair salon which they were reluctant to change. The newsroom asked us to pick up the job until we could be relieved. I liked nothing more than a hot news story, and readily agreed. It turned out to be a highly unusual and tragic event for the Isle of Man, a normally safe and tranquil place. Three people had been found dead at an isolated house in the Manx countryside. I took down the details, and we set off in search of the location. We would later discover that the parents of a severely handicapped child had killed her before committing suicide. If I'd known this at the time, I would have been better prepared for what was to come. But I didn't.

When we arrived in what I thought was the vicinity of the house we were looking for, I saw a postman delivering mail. With an intimate knowledge of the locale, this was the perfect person to ask for directions. He was having a friendly chat with a woman on her doorstep as rural postmen do, and after apologising for the interruption, I asked for his help. He directed me a quarter of a mile further on, and I thanked him and turned away. As I walked back to the car, the woman called after me, saying I should be ashamed of myself for wanting to cover such a tragic event. I said that I sympathised with her upset, but that I had a job to do. It took no more than a couple of minutes to reach the lane to the house we were looking for. But in that time, the householder must have phoned the local farmer. He arrived on the scene at the same time as us and was in no mood to be trifled with. I was used, in such circumstances, to being the focus of the anger and upset those peripherally involved felt a need to express. It's human nature to want to let it out, and I was a target of opportunity. I'd learned to roll with the metaphorical punches, and by being reasonable and sympathetic - neither of which responses under the circumstances were anything other than genuine - I would often win round the unhappy party. But it was immediately obvious there would be no chance of success from that strategy with the farmer. He told us to clear off, and that we had no right to be there. I countered by pointing out the footpath sign, explaining that it was a public right of way, and that we were free to exercise those rights. He explained that, if we did, he'd shoot us with his shotgun. I heard Eric's intake of breath beside me. Perhaps surprisingly I didn't feel in danger. If he'd reached into his vehicle, pulled out his gun and pointed it at me things might have been different. But I was in filming mode, and that created a certain level of confidence - some might say arrogance - which imbued a feeling of inviolability. There was no sign that he was surprised when I didn't immediately back down, but when I said I'd have to report his threat to the police he got back into his four-wheel drive and retreated. I produced my brick of a cell phone from a capacious anorak pocket, and for the first time ever used it to dial 999.

I was then met with a series of disappointments. I explained to the police operator that a farmer was threatening to shoot me. Her response suggested it was the sort of thing she heard every day, and twice on Saturdays. There was no element of surprise in her voice, but she promised to send someone out to us. The patch of road I was standing on fell within the responsibility of Onchan police station. The parish lies adjacent to the much larger conurbation of Douglas, where police headquarters is located. In any situation like this there's bound to be rivalry between different branches of the same organisation and, as I would find out, some relationship challenges. If the reaction to my emergency had been a let down, the arrival of the cavalry was a full blown disappointment. I'd maybe imagined an armed response unit turning up. I'd certainly expected flashing blue beacons and maybe even a bit of noise. Instead, when the police car finally arrived, it did so rather sedately. It seemed I could have drunk a cup of Earl Gray tea and read the sports section of the local paper between it appearing round the corner and coming to a halt next to us. After carefully removing their seat belts and donning their headgear, the car's two occupants unfolded themselves from their seats. It was clear this was no armed response unit. The sergeant who had so ponderously driven up the road bore an uncanny resemblance to a childhood image of PC Plod stored deep in the recesses of my memory. The PC with him looked like he had come straight from the set of an advert for acne cream in which he'd been playing the "before" role. I recall the surprise the sergeant showed when I shook his hand and introduced myself. He wasn't surprised by who I was, but rather by the act of greeting him. I explained the situation and he uttered the unforgettable words, "I'll go and sort this out." And that's what led to the next disappointment. I took his statement to mean that he would go and uphold the law, at the very least delivering a stern lecture about the seriousness of making threats to kill, and certainly enforcing our right to access the footpath. But as he and his constable disappeared down the lane towards the farmhouse, if I'd been able to read the thought bubble above his head I'd have seen he had very different ideas as to his next course of action.

Sometime around this point the associate appeared, and I have to admit their hair looked pristine. You should always look your best if you're about to get shot. I explained the lie of the land, and they didn't look too impressed. Frightened was nearer the mark. People on the Isle of Man weren't meant to come within fifty miles of a gun. This was particularly important since the island is only thirty miles from tip to toe. We hung around for a while, getting what pictures we could, awaiting the return of the island's finest. But time was our enemy, and eventually we had to leave for our next interview, which just happened to be at police headquarters.

I should take a short time out here to explain what had been going on in the farmhouse while we'd been waiting at the end of the lane. The sergeant had decided, rather than enforcing the law, to uphold a much older Manx tradition of excluding the off-comers. As an inhabitant of the mainland, or as the Manx refer to it, the adjacent island, I was an outsider. There's an ancient piece of Manx folklore involving the God Manannan. When strangers approach, Manannan is said to lay down his cloak of mist to protect the island, and the number of occasions I got stuck there because the airport was shrouded in fog bears testament to the accuracy of the legend. On this occasion, it was a different type of fog the sergeant was seeking to create. Footpaths such as the one I'd been staring at for an hour or so were overseen at that time by the Department of Highways, Ports and Properties. Our amiable sergeant, once inside the farmhouse, and perhaps sipping a nice hot cup of freshly made tea, had phoned the Department. He had decided that the best way to outsmart us and prevent me achieving my aims was by persuading them to close the footpath, thereby removing our right of access. This was where another Manx custom came into play, which is a very laudable mixture of common sense and bloody-mindedness. The official he spoke to told him to bugger off. Of course I wasn't standing around doing nothing while this was going on, and with the aid of my trusty brick-sized mobile phone I was making my own calls, one of which happened to terminate on the desk of the same official. This coincidence had little to do with any skills I may have as a journalist, being more a reflection of the diminutive size of the Manx civil service. He told me what the sergeant had tried to do, and my blood pressure rose several points. Things had now become personal.

We arrived at police headquarters, a short distance from the TT grandstand where races start and finish. We were met by John Platt, a Chief Inspector who ran the press office. John would later go on to become Deputy Chief Constable. I got on well with him, and we walked out into the sunshine together, to where we would carry out an interview about events surrounding the tragic deaths. John, like the Chief Constable, soared above six feet tall, and it was only afterwards, in view of that fact, that it struck me what I said to him might have benefited from a little finessing. "I didn't think much of your police force today," I said. He blinked in surprise at my bluntness. As I told him what had happened I saw him working harder to control his expression. When I finished, he simply said "I'll look into it." Once we'd finished filming the story we sent the tapes off to the airport, returned to our real reason for being on the island, and the events of the day soon faded. However, over the next few days we'd have regular reminders, and the size of our smiles increased with each one.

It was a another beautiful day with a warm, friendly sun beaming down from a crystal clear blue sky onto the thankful and adoring fans below. The air was filled with a sense of excitement and the aroma of hot oil as the start of the first race of that year's TT approached. Tens of thousands had descended on the island from around the world for a motorcycle spectacular, and Manannan had cast aside any surliness he might have felt from earlier in the week to lay out a stylish welcome for them. The island was looking its best, the hoteliers were counting the cash, the event organisers were praying the weather would hold, and I was wandering around the paddock area meeting old acquaintances and recruiting interviewees. It was business as usual. To describe the scene as chaotic would be reasonably accurate, yet within that overall impression there existed an intense focus. Mechanics listened closely to engines as they warmed up, searching for the slightest sound which could signal an impending mechanical failure, and riders ran a map of the course through their memory as they prepared for the excitement and danger ahead. As I scanned the sea of faces around me, there was one which, quite literally, stood out from the rest. Even if he hadn't been wearing his uniform cap, the stature of the Chief Constable ensured that he was visible above the heads of all below, and his eagle eyes had spotted me from his eyrie. We smiled a greeting at each other, and he made his way through the throng towards me, a nod of the head here and a handshake there with people as he passed by. I immediately got down to the professional stuff. "We've had some trouble this week," I said. He looked down at me, unsure of where this was going. I briefly told him the Tale of the Closed-Off Footpath and ended, "But John Platt said he'd investigate." There seemed little point in fuelling the flames much further. "Well I'm on it now too," he said, leaving no doubt that the incident was going to be dealt with seriously. We moved on to talk about the glorious weather and his tips for fancied riders in the first race before going our separate ways.

Shortly thereafter, the paddock began to empty and the circus moved onto the starting grid. We scuttled round the wall dividing the two to be faced with the bikes and riders in their starting order. For reasons of safety, competitors set off ten seconds apart, each one flagged away individually on the first lap, a 37 mile tour of the island taking in the highlights of its beauty. Not that the riders would have much opportunity to admire the view. Travelling at astonishing speeds on narrow country roads, every bit of their concentration was needed to stay away from kerbs and walls. Driving round the course in between races we'd see bales of hay stacked against trees for protection. With a touch of black humour which would doubtless be deprecated today, we'd often remark that the hay provided more protection for the trees than the riders, as many had found to their cost over the years. Amongst those lined up were some of the legendary names of the TT, multiple winners who returned each year to pit their considerable skills against course and competitors. Motorcycle racing was something I covered, at most, once a year. There were others attending the event who were infinitely more capable and knowledgeable than me. But I was always impressed with the access I was afforded. I could take my crew just about anywhere as the seconds ticked away to the start of the race and the atmosphere on the grid became calm and expectant, wandering amongst the riders, doing interviews about their strategy just moments before they set off. They were an enthusiastic and helpful bunch.

I had a well-proven routine once things got under way. The aim was to capture the race from as many different vantage points as possible. The fastest bikes completed a lap in around eighteen minutes, and I had to calculate carefully the amount of time available to move location and arrive before the first of the bikes did. It was very carefully choreographed, and although the timings were often tight, we never missed a lap. One of the regular spots we visited was Governor's Bridge, so named because it's next to the entrance to Government House, the residence of the Queen's representative on the island. Governor's Bridge is just half a mile from the end of the lap, and so it was one of the easiest places to get to while a race was under way. It's also across the boundary which separates Douglas from Onchan. We parked the vehicle and trotted past the crowd, ducking under the tape strung across the side road, and wandered along the pavement on the edge of the course. It was then that two sets of eyes interlocked. In charge of proceedings at the hairpin bend was none other than the sergeant we'd met earlier in the week. He grinned at us. "You can't film here," he said. "The road's closed." I smiled back at his humour, albeit in a somewhat wintry manner. Clearly he thought the footpath dispute was hilarious. He lowered his voice so those around us couldn't hear. "Mr Platt's been on the blower to my inspector," he said. "They're not talking now." "Good," I replied. Now it was my turn to grin. "Maybe you'll learn to uphold the law from here on." It was said with an air of jocularity, but it didn't diminish my sense of outrage at what had happened.

Two days later, we were back at the same location, and sure enough, the sergeant was in his spot once more. This time there was no grin. "Bloody hell," he groaned. "The Chief Constable's been on the phone now. He melted the line." I gave him a slow smile, but said nothing. I could see he was recalculating his responses to me. I might just be an off-comer, but I seemed to have access to a hornet's nest, and was enthusiastically poking it with a long stick. He definitely didn't want to get stung.

Covering TT was always a huge amount of hard work.

I would set up camp in a hotel on the prom in Douglas, and bring across four or five cameras and two edit suites. I once calculated that I'd worked more than a hundred and thirty of the hundred and sixty eight hours in the week. It was utterly exhausting, and I'd regularly be ill when I got back home. But in amongst all of the work there was one highlight of the week I'd look forward to. It was a chance to relax for a couple of hours at the Governor's TT garden party. Peter Kneale, the jovial press officer who was a walking encyclopaedia of knowledge about the event, and who doubled up by hosting Manx Radio's excellent race commentary, ensured we got an invitation to consume canapés and champagne - and rather a lot of gin and tonic - while we watched the Red Arrows display overhead. It was only as we drove into the entrance to Government House that it occurred to me that we were back in Onchan. Almost as soon as I made the connection, I saw on the driveway in front of us the sting-averse sergeant. Our eyes locked again, and it was as if we could all read his mind. A look of frozen terror crossed his face, transmitting his greatest fear. This time, the thought bubble above his head was perfectly legible. It read, "Oh no! First he complained about me to the Chief Inspector. Then he went to the Chief Constable. Now he's going to report me to the Governor!"

As the garden party went on, there were many bemused glances cast in our direction as other guests speculated about why we seemed to be spending the entire evening laughing uproariously. It turns out revenge isn't sweet after all. It tastes of expensive, well chilled champagne. And it's delicious.

An important part of the job of Oliver, from the Central Office of Information, was to act as sheepdog, rounding up the press pack and keeping them in order. And so it was that he collected our group, now full of some very pleasant sandwiches, and ushered us into a mini-bus to head for the afternoon destination. The Princess Royal was to open Carlisle's newest amenity, the Sands Centre. A multi-purpose venue, it was designed to serve both the sporting and entertainment needs of the city. The red brick building is just a few hundred yards from the magnificent 12th century castle, and immediately next to one of Carlisle's other most prominent features, the Hardwick Circus roundabout. This giant of construction, surely visible from space, is as puzzling as it is huge, standing at the end of an isolated short stretch of dual carriageway which was inexplicably allowed to create a barrier between castle and city. Bonnie Prince Charlie would never have been able to take control of Carlisle Castle if the city fathers had thought to build a dual carriageway around it in 1745. Plans to extend the road somewhere useful never materialised, so it and its monstrous carbuncle of a roundabout commemorate a civic ambition unfulfilled. We almost needed a further supply of sandwiches to sustain us as we set out on the long and tedious journey around it.

Some might argue that roundabouts like Hardwick Circus are a kind of divine retribution for the invention of the motor car. I once met a man who had been part of the team who designed Milton Keynes new town. It's laid out using a grid pattern of main roads, a kilometre apart, with a roundabout at each of the main intersections. The little known secret about their size is intriguing, if slightly comical. When the civil engineers were working on their plan they had no trouble drawing the roads. They were simple straight lines. But the roundabouts needed to be circular, and that meant finding something that was both round and the correct size. They cast around the office for what was available. He didn't reveal why the drawing office didn't have a compass, but what it did possess a-plenty was tea cups. So an empty one was up-ended, and a pencil used to draw the required circles around its circumference. Strange, but true. By extrapolation, the designers of Hardwick Circus presumably used a dustbin lid. It's huge. With a small park in its centre, it's similar in concept to Dupont Circle in Washington, DC. That's named after a Rear Admiral who served during the American Civil War, Samuel Francis Du Pont, and I've had the dubious pleasure of interacting with it. I came upon it without any prior knowledge of the challenge it presented, and departed a defeated man. Dupont Circle connects no fewer than nine roads. One of them, Connecticut Avenue, leads to The White House, less than a mile away. Fans of the television series The West Wing will recall an episode where President Bartlet's press secretary, C J Cregg, gets caught up there in traffic on the way to work. I can understand how. The circle is actually two large concentric roundabouts, one inside the other. But while the outside one connects to all of the intersecting roads, the inside one only allows access to about half. Unwittingly, I entered the inside loop and found to my confusion that I couldn't get off on the road I wanted. I felt like a giant hamster trapped in a wheel, and it took three rotations before I eventually worked out how to escape.

Dupont also provided me with one of many episodes of synchronicity, a concept first described by Austrian psychologist Carl Jung as *meaningful coincidences*. I had two interviews to do at different buildings either side of lunch. As we set up in a room overlooking the Circle, I glanced out of the floor to ceiling window and saw a man hail a cab. He was standing on the narrow pedestrian median which separates the two concentric roundabouts, and when his yellow ride pulled up he attempted to open the back door to get in. After the third or fourth failed effort to gain entry, the driver got out and guided him through the complex technology. I was amused by the scene, its visual humour reminiscent of a scene from a Laurel and Hardy movie. But there was a faint recognition, something about the cack-handedness of this man's body language that rang a bell in my mind. I watched the cab as it snaked around the traffic lanes before disappearing off towards its destination, searching the depths of my memory for a connection I couldn't quite recall. It eventually came to me. I'd met him on a previous visit, and on that occasion too, he'd seemed strangely at odds with the physical world. He was one of the army of Washington lobbyists, and I'd gone to interview him about world food poverty at the end of a long filming trip in the US. It was the last day of the shoot, and I was tired. As Eric and his sound recordist set up our equipment for the interview, I took a moment to plan the conversation ahead, trying hard to keep my eyes open. From my position, I could see out to the thickly carpeted reception area. On the wall was a series of four shelves, arranged one above the other. They were angled at forty-five degrees with a small lip on the lower edge so that the displayed back numbers of the organisation's magazine could be seen clearly by visitors. My interviewee had stepped out of his office to allow us to prepare and, on his way to whatever it was he was going to do for a few minutes, his attention was drawn to the shelves. Perhaps he had mild OCD, because he decided that the arrangement of the publications was not precisely to his liking. He spent five minutes or so carefully rearranging them, ensuring that the horizontal spacing was exactly equal, and that each shelf's magazines were in line with those above and below. Finally, satisfied with his work, he padded away around the corner. But no sooner had he disappeared from sight than about a third of the magazines jumped off the shelves and landed silently on the thick carpet below, undoing his patient work in a trice. It was another Laurel and Hardy moment, but one that I alone had been a witness to. It was this physical ineptitude I'd seen in his struggle with the cab door, an unusual foible which made him so memorable.

When I finished the first interview above Dupont we

had an hour and a half to kill. We visited a bookshop just off the Circle where Eric found and promptly bought a book about his hero, Warren Buffett. It was very big and heavy, and I worried about him breaching his baggage allowance on the flight home. We then traversed the roundabout to find lunch in a pleasant delicatessen. After forty minutes or so, suitably fortified, we left and headed back to the car in its underground parking garage. We'd eaten no more than a hundred yards from Dupont Circle, and as we walked back towards it down 19th Street, I glanced into a coffee shop on my right. To my astonishment I saw Taxi Man standing at the counter. Within the space of less than two hours I'd now seen the only person I knew in the nation's capital, not once, but twice. I find these bits of synchronicity haunt me on a regular basis. They're a fascination, bringing people together in time and space in a way which echoes Jung's definitive requirement of being both coincidental and meaningful.

The navigation of Hardwick Circus bore none of the difficulties of Dupont, and we disembarked from the mini-bus in the Sands Centre car park. We were carefully watched by an enthusiastic crowd awaiting the Princess Royal's arrival, and one or two waved in excitement. A raised platform had been set up with a curtained-off plaque situated at the back, suitably inscribed with the date and details of the opening. Oliver explained that Princess Anne would make a short speech before officially opening the building by unveiling the plaque. It was the first of two small, but important things which wouldn't go to plan. The Princess arrived and the crowd cheered and waved their tiny Union Jacks. She shook a few hands before ascending the steps to the platform. But, instead of heading for the microphone, without any warning she tugged at the cord which opened the little pair of curtains. The Sands Centre had been rather unceremoniously opened without any of the expected pomp. Unfortunately, as things stood, the world was not going to be informed of the occasion, because the camera hadn't been running. Such had been the speed at which she'd moved, Eric had, very unusually, been caught unawares. There was one consolation, though. Bobby, the BBC's cameraman, had also missed the tug of the cord. What could have been an embarrassment for us, had Bobby captured what we missed, now called for a solution which would save everyone's collective neck.

Princess Anne and her accompanying party made off towards the entrance for a tour of the building, and I leapt into action. As a now puzzled crowd looked on, I mounted the podium and took off my jacket before rolling up a sleeve. I carefully pulled the curtains closed again and told both cameramen to roll, their cameras focussed tightly on where the plaque would appear. I counted to five, then leaned in and gave the cord a firm pull. The curtains opened, and we could now announce to the world that the Sands Centre had been officially opened. I swear there was a smattering of applause from the crowd. I rolled my sleeve back down, put on my jacket, and we trotted off in hot pursuit of the

Royal party. It may have been the haste of our arrival in the building which caused the problem, but what came next led to the second unplanned incident, albeit one which Eric treasures to this day. Oliver explained the route the group would take on their tour, and we positioned ourselves accordingly. We seemed to have made a good recovery from the earlier debacle, and I was confident we'd get some good pictures from close at hand of Princess Anne inspecting the facilities she had so ably, if rather unexpectedly opened. Quite how close those pictures would turn out to be, I couldn't have anticipated. We had just set off through the building with Eric hand-holding the camera on his shoulder when she unexpectedly appeared round a corner in front of him. He pressed the start button and began to film, backing away to keep a respectful distance between himself and Her Royal Highness. She in turn didn't look at the camera, and continued talking with the local dignitaries accompanying her. Clearly, she'd been on the course. Everything was going splendidly. Until, that is, Eric ran out of corridor. Suddenly, he felt a wall behind him as the route through the building took a ninety-degree turn. He pressed his body into the corner as hard as he could, but with the camera on his shoulder and its long lens protruding forward, there simply wasn't enough space for Princess Anne to get past. Eric opened his left eye - the one not looking through the eyepiece - and treated her to his party trick. But it wasn't enough to defuse the situation. For what seemed like an eternity, they stared at each other, neither prepared to move or speak. Finally, Princess

Anne blinked first. In what was a unique occasion for any of the press party that day, the Princess spoke to Eric. The words have stayed with him since then, indelibly etched in his memory. Slowly and precisely, with a clarity to be expected from one so accustomed to making public speeches - though sadly not on that particular afternoon - she issued her Royal observation. "You appear," she said, looking directly at Eric's single visible eye, "to be in my way." As Royal conversations go, it wasn't the most notable. It won't be found in some great archive devoted to the British Royal Family. But the observation was entirely accurate, and those seven little words are remembered by Eric with enormous pride. His camera could well have sported a prominent label from that moment on, reading "Eric Scott-Parker - by Appointment to HRH The Princess Royal". And Oliver's words were almost as memorable. "She wasn't supposed to go that way."

I stayed behind in the newsroom after the programme went out that evening for curiosity's sake, but the phone stayed silent. We'd edited the film to give the appearance that we had indeed captured the moment Her Royal Highness had drawn back the curtains to reveal the plaque. It was a tiny subterfuge, but one I thought I could justify. And it looked like we'd got away with it. But I remain confused about how we did, and can only come up with two possible explanations. Either that night's audience was somehow distracted en-masse at the vital moment, or the British public is supremely content with the idea that Princess Anne has an unusually hairy arm.

THE MANX SECRET
NUCLEAR DUMP

The view from the fell road above Calder Bridge in West Cumbria beckons you to stop and breathe in its tranquillity as you pass. There's almost a set of tripod marks permanently inset in the ground from the times I've filmed from here, immersed in the beauty of the location. The vantage point is high, overlooking an area which has played an important role in the country's industrial and social history. Below is the village of Thornhill, just a mile or two from the Irish Sea. It was a new community built in the 1920s to fulfil a national promise to provide improved housing for those who'd returned from war. To the right lies the 13th century market town of Egremont. Some may recognise it as the host of the annual Crab Fair, which encompasses the World Gurning Championships and the sport of greasy pole climbing, both events surely the favourites of politicians everywhere. But Egremont has a more important claim to fame, and one which underlines why West Cumbria's place in history is so important. Just south of the town is Florence Mine, the last deep iron ore mine in Europe until it closed in 2008. And often when you find iron there's coal nearby. The towns of Whitehaven and Workington lie just over the fells to the north, each having played its part in developing the nation. The people around here are second to none. They hewed coal from deep underground to stoke the fires of the Industrial Revolution, and were the first to produce commercial quantities of mild rolled steel rails, still found on railway tracks around the world. As an added bonus, when the sun shines and the air is clear this spot offers a view of a jewel standing out across the water. The Isle of Man is a little over thirty miles away, but on a crisp day it seems like you can reach out and touch it. Sandwiched in between is Britain's biggest and dirtiest nuclear site. Sellafield.

Sellafield occupies a position on one of the least appreciated coastlines in Britain. The Irish Sea laps beautiful, golden beaches which cry out to be explored. But at times those who take their exercise here have been subjected to a threat from some pretty nasty radio-nuclides. The currents, strong enough to reshape the sandy dunes which are home to half of the UK's population of Natterjack toads, have spread contamination around much of northern Europe. The nuclear reprocessing site was once called Windscale, but after a series of radioactive leaks the name became as toxic as the Plutonium it deals with and was initially designed to produce. So a PR campaign swung into action to expunge the damaging name from the public's memory, and a new name was invented.

There was a very clever press officer who worked here. Jake Kelly was a former BBC news reporter who was lured to go and work for British Nuclear Fuels, which ran much of the site. Jake was a pleasant guy to deal with, and coped well with the pressures he must have felt during a particularly bad period when the site seemed to leak radioactivity on a regular basis. I lost count of the number of times we'd head there for yet another story. But Jake turned things to his advantage. Instead of the culture of secrecy which had previously existed, he issued a press release for even the smallest of problems. At first it seemed a refreshing approach, and each was eagerly devoured and disseminated. But after a while there grew a weariness of their inevitability and slowly the site began to drop out of the news, which was exactly what Jake had planned.

Many governments objected to Sellafield's presence over the years, amongst them the ever-visible Isle of Man. But even as its lawmakers continue to express their worries about the effect of the site's activities on their marine ecology, a small reminder of another country's history in the development of nuclear weapons lies hidden and unknown in the unlikely setting of a housing estate on the south of the island, thousands of miles from the desert where it was created in a fraction of a second by a nuclear test explosion. This is the story, told for the very first time, of how it got to be there and exactly what it is. This is the story of the Manx secret nuclear dump.

The Second World War was brought to an end when two Atomic bombs were dropped on Japan. The events were the culmination of an incredible engineering exercise which began when Italian physicist Enrico Fermi carried out an experiment on the floor of a racquets court at the University of Chicago in December 1942. It confirmed that the energy produced by splitting the atom could be controlled. Many decades later I stood at the same spot, now marked by an impressive Henry Moore sculpture, and marvelled at Mankind's ability to promote self-destruction. But I felt as though I was in possession of secret knowledge as I stood admiring it. Here I was at the place which changed the world, yet those who passed me by paid little or no attention to Moore's masterpiece, set in the middle of a slightly raised paved area close to its commemorative plaque.

A few days earlier, at a site off Highway 26 near Arco in Idaho's high desert, I felt touched by history. I was standing in front of a display case in a tiny museum which contained two priceless artefacts. The first was a Chianti bottle, opened by Eugene Wigner to celebrate the experiment's success, and signed by all those present. The second was a small notebook used by Fermi to record the increase in radioactivity as the cadmium control rods were slowly and carefully removed from the pile, inching towards a position which would allow it to achieve a self-sustaining chain reaction. I read his handwritten notes which showed the experiment progressing well. But at about midday, just as the reactor pile was about to reach the point of criticality when the answer to the question they all sought would be answered, he ordered that the rods' positions be marked, before being reinserted to bring the reaction to a halt. Fermi had decided it was time for lunch.

After a very pleasant repast lasting two hours they returned, and at 2:32 pm a pencilled entry proclaimed their success. This group of learned scientists, whose curiosity seemed to have no bounds, had let the genie slip from the bottle. There followed a phone call between Arthur Compton, Chairman of the committee established to explore the feasibility of an Atomic bomb, and James Conant, Chairman of the National Defense Research Committee. Compton began the conversation, aware that secrecy was of the utmost importance on the unsecured line. He spoke carefully and precisely. "The Italian Navigator has landed in the New World." An excited Conan replied, "Were the natives friendly?" to which the answer came, "Everyone landed safe and happy."

In a plain, air-conditioned room just off Genesee Avenue in La Jolla, north of San Diego, I sat opposite a man who was dressed casually in a ribbed sweater and open necked shirt. Were it not for the location, he might have seemed like someone's grandfather, come to check on a granddaughter's or grandson's progress at work. But appearances were wildly deceptive. This was, after all, one of the highest-tech areas of California. Close by was the University of California, San Diego with the Scripps Institution of Oceanography nestling on its beachfront campus. The Salk Institute was less than a mile south-west, founded by the developer of the first polio vaccine, Jonas Salk. To the east, the mighty Interstate I-5, one of the major arteries of the west coast, thundered by with Qualcomm, the company which invented a military communications system which became the basis for 3G mobile phones, just beyond. The military presence was in plain sight. Miramar, the Marine Corps air base made famous by the Tom Cruise film *Top Gun*, lay five miles south-east. The Marine Corps' massive Camp Pendleton was to the north, and the home of the US Pacific Fleet to the south in San Diego.

The man was Harold Agnew, and we were sitting in the offices of General Atomics. Agnew's name is not one that instantly springs to mind as an innovator, but the story he had to tell was rooted deep in nuclear history. He had lugged around bricks of Graphite and Uranium, building the reactor pile on the floor of the court under instruction from Fermi. And at the age of 21 he had stood on the observation gallery above as the experiment progressed to the point of success. Talking with him, hearing him describe events, was akin to being there myself. The atmosphere was electric as the interview progressed, and I sat transfixed by his story and his modesty. At Los Alamos, deep amongst the New Mexico canyons, he ran a particle accelerator programme to refine the Atomic bomb's design. And on 6th August 1945 when the B-29 bomber Enola Gay took off to drop the Little Boy weapon on Hiroshima, he was on board, ready to film the devastation with a Bell & Howell 16 mm camera. Harold Agnew was unique, the only person to witness developments from racquets court to detonation.

Fermi's experiment had led to an event at 5:45 am on 16th July 1945 which would change the world forever. At a site in the New Mexico desert at Alamogordo, just before the sun rose to provide warmth to a group of expectant scientists and observers, their faces were instead touched by the heat from the first Atomic explosion. A huge mushroom cloud rose into the still air as The Gadget, hoisted to the top of a 100 feet high tower, performed flawlessly. The Trinity Test showed that Atomic weapons were more than theoretical. Yet despite the involvement of British scientists in the early work, the McMahon Act, which came into force on January 1st 1947, prohibited the sharing of America's nuclear secrets with foreign powers, no matter how instrumental they had been in helping with the realisation of the Atomic bomb. So Britain began its own work to create a nuclear weapon, and the site at Windscale was central to it. Two 400 feet high chimneys were built above Graphite reactors, not dissimilar from those Fermi had designed in Chicago. Their purpose was to produce Plutonium, a vital element for what became known as the nuclear deterrent.

The Arms Race was now well under way, with the Americans, British and Russians out in front. In November 1952 the United States carried out its first Hydrogen bomb test, an act which destroyed the atoll upon which it took place. The weapon had been heavily promoted by Hungarian-American theoretical physicist Edward Teller, thought to have been the inspiration for the fictional character Dr. Strangelove. He was a difficult, often volatile character, and his proposal for a thermo-nuclear weapon was opposed by many of his contemporaries who didn't believe it would work. His reputation was well earned, and he is probably the most frightening man I have ever interviewed.

I met Teller a few short years before his death. The first words he uttered to me were, "I didn't want to do this interview." But rather than be despondent about his attitude, I actually felt buoyed. After all, I was standing in his office, and had got there only by reason of a determination that I wasn't going to allow him to slip through my grasp.

At the time, I was making a programme about the 1957 fire in one of the Windscale reactors built to produce fissile material for Britain's Atomic bomb. The fire was caused by a build-up and subsequent release of stored energy in the Graphite pile. This cyclical effect had been documented by one of Teller's colleagues, a fellow Hungarian scientist, Eugene Wigner. By now Wigner was dead, so I looked upon Teller as the next best person to provide a concise explanation of how the fire had come about. I traced him to an office in the Hoover Tower on the campus of Stanford University, south of San Francisco. His assistant, a lovely lady called Patti, listened to me as I explained what I wanted to do, and was kind enough to give me his home phone number and an agreed time at which I should call. At the appointed hour - 7 pm GMT, 11 am PST - I left the family watching television to make the call from the kitchen, and nervously dialled his number. My training as a television news reporter has provided me with an armoury of techniques which I find useful in a whole variety of different situations. On the phone to Teller, I automatically adopted an approach I had developed for reluctant interviewees.

There are few things better designed to get your attention than seeing the clock on the newsroom wall tick round as you desperately try to make your story stand up. Your crew is sitting, feet up in the camera room, hoping against hope that you're going to fail, thereby giving them a quiet morning. The programme editor is sitting behind you, casting a glance of irritation every few minutes because you still haven't left the building. Meanwhile, having tried half a dozen potential interviewees to discover that they're not answering their phone, are in a meeting, or out of the country on holiday, I have latched on to the one person I could actually get hold of, and I'm not planning on letting them escape without agreeing to see me. It was this war of attrition I used on Teller. He was too polite to hang up on me, and I relied on him continuing to have an intellectual argument about why he didn't want me to fly five and a half thousand miles to see him. He was, after all, a scientist, and scientists are logical people. So he was trying to logic his way out of doing an interview. What he didn't appreciate was that I'd done the course. A long time previously, with a different employer on a different career path, I had learned a little about the psychology of selling. I wasn't great at it, but I was good enough. So, for forty-five minutes I wore him down. In the end I don't know whether he wanted to go for lunch or head for the loo, but he reluctantly capitulated to my demands. I felt triumphant as I put the phone down. Edward Teller, here I come. And it was this meeting with Teller which led directly to the small piece of nuclear history arriving on the Isle of Man.

While Teller was promoting his Hydrogen bomb ideas there were those who saw another use for this new source of energy. In December 1953 President Eisenhower presented his Atoms for Peace speech at the United Nations General Assembly. Thinking turned to designing power stations which produced electricity from nuclear fission. The concept, if not the implementation, was relatively simple. The heat from the reaction produced steam which powered a turbine, and that in turn rotated a generator to create electricity. The first demonstration of this new use for fission came about rather hurriedly. The Americans discovered that their Cold War enemies were about to make an announcement about peaceful uses for nuclear energy at the Geneva Summit on 18th July 1955. The meeting between the big four powers was designed to reduce international tensions, and those attending included US President Dwight D. Eisenhower, British PM Anthony Eden with Harold Macmillan, French Prime Minister Edgar Faure, and Soviet Premier Nicolai Bulganin, along with Vyacheslav Molotov and Nikita Khrushchev. The eyes of the world would be on the conference and the Americans were determined not to be outmanoeuvred. Engineers at a nuclear test site in Idaho were tasked with beating the Russians to the punch. The site is to nuclear reactors what Boston, Massachusetts is to education. I was told by someone in that city that there are more universities and colleges within a 25 mile radius than in any comparable area elsewhere else in the world. With no fewer than fifty nuclear reactors within its 900 square mile area, the Idaho site makes a similar boast. BORAX-III, a boiling water reactor, was used for the demonstration, and power lines were laid across the desert to the city of Arco, population 995.

On a hot summer afternoon, I chatted with a retired electrician as he pruned fruit bushes in his garden in nearby Idaho Falls ahead of a violent thunderstorm approaching from the west. He was a quiet, unassuming man. To look at him, you would never guess the vital role he played in giving the United States the upper hand at the Geneva Summit. Ray Haroldsen had been late to the top secret project. The United States had already had its fingers burned when British scientist Klaus Fuchs leaked secrets from the Manhattan Project to the Russians during the Second World War. So security around the BORAX-III test couldn't have been higher, and Ray's involvement was delayed by two weeks while he waited for his clearance to come through. He proudly explained how he'd solved a problem the team didn't even know they had. In a constant voltage generator, a secondary circuit known as an exciter is used to power the electromagnetic field, and when Ray was eventually allowed access he discovered that it was this circuit which was powering the four light bulbs being used as a temporary load. In his words, it had been wired up backwards. So he set about correcting the mistake, and on 17th July 1955, electricity flowed across the desert and into Arco, just a day before the Geneva Summit.

The folks in Arco are quite excited about the part they played in the history of nuclear power. It's a tiny community, and as I drove in from the south-east, one of the first buildings I saw was a restaurant which proudly advertised itself as the home of the Atomic Burger. A large sign around the corner on US-93 commemorates that event in 1955 when, probably for the first and last time, Arco led the world. It was, almost literally, Arco's fifteen minutes of fame. In fact it lasted for sixty minutes, until the power lines, delivering a current way beyond what they were designed for, burned out and fell to the desert floor. But that wasn't important. This little city had provided a glimpse of the future.

A year or so later Queen Elizabeth II opened Calder Hall, the world's first commercial nuclear power station. Or at least that's what everyone was told. Somebody, their identity now lost in history, was quoted as saying that it would produce electricity too cheap to meter. But the power it generated was little more than a by-product. Calder Hall's real purpose was to make Plutonium.

At some point along the way, the idea came about that the processes developed at Windscale could be employed to make money by re-processing spent nuclear fuel from countries around the world. In so many ways it was a disastrous political mistake which linked civil nuclear energy with the technology's military purposes. It led to the famous Daily Mirror headline on 21st October 1975 which set the tone for decades to come, claiming that Britain was becoming the world's nuclear dustbin.

When I began reporting on activities at Sellafield, its purpose was something of a mystery, at least as far as I was concerned. There was a confusing cacophony of strident voices, each with its own story, each with its own agenda. The western edge of Sellafield lies close to the waters of the Irish Sea, and the main gate here was usually where we'd enter the site. We'd park outside the reception building before going through the long process of signing in. Eventually, someone from the press office would arrive to escort us onto the site. Often we'd get no further than the building that housed the press staff, but that in itself was always a treat. It had a type of lift I'd never seen before. A paternoster. It had no sliding doors which opened to allow you in before you were whisked to the floor of your choosing. This was much more fun. It consisted of a continuously moving collection of cars which ascended on one side of the shaft and descended on the other. Like an escalator, it required a deft technique to step into a car as its floor reached the level of the floor you were on, and similarly good timing to step out of it when you arrived at the floor where you wanted to get off. The film crew spoke in awe of one electrician who'd stayed on board and gone over the top before beginning the descent on the other side. I never found the courage to try it myself, and had nightmares about what would happen to me if I missed getting off at the ground floor on the way down.

It seemed that Sellafield and I didn't get on well when it came to moving between floors. One particular building which always seemed to cause us problems was THORP, the Thermal Oxide Reprocessing Plant. Designed to make money from reprocessing nuclear fuel from the UK and elsewhere, it largely failed to live up to its commercial promise, and I seemed to visit it on a regular basis for one story or another. It was a tall building, and we inevitably needed to be on the top floor. But an odd thing happened each time we arrived there to film, and it wasn't long before I sensed a pattern to the behaviour. As we entered through the doorway, the press officer escorting us would turn and explain that the lifts were out of commission that day and we'd have to use the stairs. So we'd set off up six or seven flights of stairs lugging our heavy equipment with us. By the time we reached the top, work was the last thing on our minds. It happened so regularly that I suspected we were being played, but had no proof to support my theory. That would only come twenty years later when I ran into someone I thought I recognised. Mike Smith had been in charge of THORP for a period, and once I'd completed the interview I'd come to do with him, we began to chat informally. I asked him about the building's lifts, and told him we'd found them to be particularly unreliable. I suppose I shouldn't have been surprised by his response. He gave me an emphatic "No," explaining that they were required to have the lifts operational at all times for getting vital equipment where it was needed. When I told him of my many climbs up the stairs he found it hilarious. I can only assume that this was the press office's way of getting back at us for the negative stories we did about the place. But I suppose everyone's entitled to inject a little humour into their job. Even if it is at our expense.

The third lift I met at Sellafield was actually a hoist. It was designed to transport men and materials 410 feet up to the top of one of the Windscale Pile chimneys when it was being decommissioned. The day I travelled in it is one I won't easily forget. It was during the making of the programme about the 1957 fire which led me to Edward Teller. It's a fascinating story of missed opportunity, happenstance and incredible bravery. The two Windscale Piles were constructed of high purity Graphite, with the fuel elements and control rods inserted horizontally into channels which ran all the way from front to back. To this day, some aspects of the accident remain secret, and as I stood looking at the reactor face I was met with a straight refusal when I asked someone to point out the area where the fire had started. There was a fundamental flaw in its design, and the physics had been described by Teller's colleague Eugene Wigner. Teller had mentioned the dangers of a fire in a graphite reactor to scientists at Harwell during a visit in 1948, but his information wasn't followed up. Perhaps the British nuclear physicists disagreed with him. Perhaps the conversation became lost in a highly technical exchange. Or perhaps Teller's warning was ignored because acquiring the Plutonium necessary for an Atomic weapon was simply too important to allow anything to get in the way. Whatever the reason, the danger was shown to be much more than theoretical.

I travelled to California to meet with Teller and have him explain, in language that a layman could understand, exactly what went wrong. His office was in the Hoover Tower, a magnificent domed structure which sits on the beautiful campus of Stanford University. I had been to Stanford before, and I'm very fond of this incredible seat of learning. Founded by railroad tycoon Leland Stanford, it was completed a few years before the great San Francisco earthquake of 1906. In the quadrangle, engraved diamond-shaped pavers commemorate the graduation of each year's students, with the one for the year of the earthquake cut in half to acknowledge the damage and disruption it caused. Teller was eating lunch when we arrived, so I chatted with his assistant

Patti while we waited for him to finish. There's a truism that you never get a second opportunity to create a first impression. Time is a cruel master and distorts the image of people through a combination of their physical decline and your own unconscious prejudices. I have often looked at war heroes who flew their Spitfires in aerial battles during the Second World War, struggling to see within them the young warrior they once were. This is how it was with Teller. It was as though I was being given preferential access to a private side of his life I had no business seeing. The room had a stale smell of someone else's food, an odour that was both unpalatable and unpleasant. The man sat in what could only be described as the senior's equivalent of a high chair, with the table set close to his chest to catch any falling morsels. Patti cleared the plates and I shook hands with the great man. It was then that he uttered that memorable greeting. "I never wanted to do this interview." But the moment passed and we exchanged pleasantries for a short period, which I found unusually hard work. Eventually I suggested he might have some work to do while we set up the equipment.

While he was out of the room, the cameraman who had accompanied me did an extraordinary thing. On the wall behind Teller's desk was a large blackboard, and chalked on it was an equation, the longest and most complex I had ever seen. I'm sure it solved some mathematical problem, but it meant nothing to me. Mike stepped up to it and wet his finger, before rubbing out one of the numbers. He then picked up the chalk and wrote a different digit in its place. I can only imagine how catastrophic the effect of this change might have been, with the possibilities ranging from the next Hydrogen bomb failing to work to Teller's weekly grocery bill not balancing. Mike and I shared a look, but I said nothing. There was an expression approaching triumphalism in his eyes, the sort of look which says "I've just got something over him". I never did ask his reasons for altering that formula, but I'm confident there are psychologists who would be happy to charge a lot of money to investigate. Once the interview was complete, a repeat of the surreptitious chalking returned the formula to how it had been.

Teller was very limiting in what he was prepared to talk about. There was no enthusiasm for debate about the ethics of his work, or to talk in any wider context about his involvement with the Manhattan Project. It was frustrating to say the least. But on the science he was unbeatable, and explained concisely, in his strong accent, the cause of the fire. The problem with air-cooled reactors of the design used at Windscale was their low operating temperature. When the nuclear reaction took place it released energy. Some of it was captured and stored by the pile's Graphite core as atoms forming its crystalline structure were displaced. This is known as Wigner Energy, named after Teller's Hungarian colleague who had discovered it. It was important that the energy be released in a controlled manner to avoid large temperature spikes. This task was undertaken in a process known as annealing, when the temperature of the reactor was raised significantly, encouraging the stored energy to be released as the atoms returned to their original state. The next generation of Magnox reactors were cooled by carbon dioxide and ran at more than double the temperature. This caused them to be self-annealing, and the danger posed by Wigner Energy was no longer a problem. But with the Windscale Piles the process had to be carried out manually.

By October 1957, the reactor team had learned a lot about the technique required, although it had been observed the process was becoming more difficult, and the temperature at which the energy was released had been increasing. On the morning of 10th October the process was begun, but this time it didn't go according to plan. Most of the reactor behaved as it should, but one channel continued to experience a rise in temperature. British scientists lacked the experience of their American and Russian counterparts, and were still learning the practicalities of Plutonium production. Additionally, the design of the reactor's instrumentation was flawed. Each thermocouple which measured temperature was shared between a number of channels, and this lack of granularity proved fatal. With insufficient information available to the operators, the rising temperature went unnoticed and the reactor caught fire, threatening to turn a large area of north-west England into a nuclear wasteland.

The reactor manager was a man called Tom Tuohy. It was to be his bravery and determination which saved the day. That's not to say that others didn't play their part, but Tom took on the role of some sort of comic book hero. He told me his tale in the sitting room of his house in West Cumbria. I had been in the research phase of the Windscale programme, talking to anyone with knowledge of the accident, and deciding who I should interview and where I should film. I called Tom late one afternoon, and as we spoke on the phone it quickly became obvious that he would be one of the central characters in the programme. I asked if we could arrange to come and see him, and he told me he was going overseas the following day, and would be away for some time. I was desperate not to let him disappear off to some far-flung corner of the world, and persuaded him to allow me to come and interview him that evening. I rounded up a crew, and we set off for what would be an evening to remember.

I have become adept over the years at categorising people very quickly. When you only have an hour or two in someone's company, assessing their importance to a story becomes second nature. I used to play a game with my main cameraman, Eric, on the often long drive from one interviewee to the next. We'd compare notes about the person we'd just met, and discuss our views of what they'd said. Each of us had a different perspective. Looking through the viewfinder of his camera gave Eric a much more focussed view, which excluded any extraneous distractions and allowed him to - I suppose the best word is stare - in a way that would be otherwise socially unacceptable. I on the other hand sought to make what I have always regarded as a data connection with the other person's brain, reaching inside to abstract the relevant information. It was a fragile connection, and in a hyper-aware state I would constantly be sensing for any sound or movement which could interrupt the flow and destroy the moment. It felt like I was hanging on to a cliff edge by my fingernails, and the slightest movement could cause me to slip. A good interviewer listens very carefully to what is being said and reacts accordingly. There's a tendency amongst some to try to show off their knowledge, and whilst many interviews can be conversations, for what I wanted to capture my presence in what would end up on air was not required. I subscribed very firmly to the thinking of Radio One DJ John Peel. He said that the role of a radio presenter was equivalent to the numbers on the pages of a book, there only for guidance. That was the way I felt about my role. I'd also invented a one sentence guide to my programme making ethos. I argued that it was my job to provide a lens on the world rather than a filter.

Of course, while I was sitting there concentrating intensely on the intellectual dance which was taking place, I knew that Eric had my back. Unusually perhaps for a cameraman, he paid attention to what was being said. A long time previously it had helped save the day. He'd been working at that time as an assistant cameraman with a different director, making a programme on the ferry which crossed the Irish Sea from Stranraer in the far south-west of Scotland to Larne in Northern Ireland. It had been a long and tiring day, and there was just one final task to complete, an interview with the head of the ferry company on the stern of the ship as it began the journey back to Scotland, with Larne slowly receding in the background. The production was being made on film then, and the first thing to do when the director called for the camera to roll was to mark the shot using a clapper board. This allowed the editor to synchronise sound with pictures in the edit suite. Eric clapped the board and settled himself down to wait out the interview, his mind beginning to anticipate dinner and all that entailed. He picked up the piece of chalk which was used to record the shot information on the slate and wrote "Drinks?" on the back before showing it to the sound recordist Cliff. He got a smile and an enthusiastic nod in return. The interview droned on, and although the idea of a tasty steak and a few drams of whisky was now foremost in his mind, a part of his brain continued to multi-task, listening to what was being said. Which was just as well in the circumstances, because everyone else had switched off completely by the time the mistake was made. The interviewer asked the head of the ferry company, "What's your over-riding aim in dealing with your passengers?" The interviewee saw this as an invitation to self-promote. In a confident voice he announced "At Sealink we always set out to make our passengers' journeys as inconvenient as possible, and to make the crossing as uncomfortable as we can." As the alarms bells rang in Eric's brain, the interviewer moved on to ask the next question, seemingly oblivious to his interviewee's gaffe in saying exactly the opposite of what he had meant. Eric looked around at the other faces. The production assistant was busy taking notes, the sound recordist was concentrating on maintaining the correct sound level, and the director gave Eric a smile which portrayed an expression of supreme innocence. Even the interviewer gave no sign that he was aware of what had been said. Eventually, the interview came to a natural end, and the director called "Cut!" The words "Well done" and "Excellent" were heard several times before Eric spoke up. He said to the ferry boss, "Excuse me. Do you know what you said in the interview about service standards?" The man looked at him with some astonishment. "Of course," he replied. "I said we help make the passengers' journeys as convenient as possible, and ensure the crossing is very comfortable." Eric explained what he'd heard. The man snorted. "Don't be ridiculous! I wouldn't be so stupid as to say something like that." Eric turned to Cliff and said, "Can you wind the tape back and play that section of the interview so we can all be sure?" Cliff grumbled a little, but did as he was asked, and the boss' face went white. He was distraught. "Please can we do it again?" he pleaded. "I'll be sacked if you let that go out." And so it was agreed that they would ask that question again. Everyone resumed their position, and the director called for the camera to roll once more. Eric stepped in, and held up the clapper board to mark the beginning of the take. The ferry boss, now slightly shaken by his performance, looked at the back of it and saw Eric's previously scribbled question to Cliff. "Drinks?" His immediate reaction was one of misinterpretation. He turned to Eric and said, "Yes. Yes. Of course. And a meal. A steak. Anything you want!" A very jolly time was had for the remainder of the journey, and there was much relieved laughter as the drink flowed at the ferry company's expense, all because of Eric's keen attention to detail, and that small matter of a misunderstanding over the chalked question on the back of the clapper board.

Tom Tuohy seemed easy to work out. He fitted into a group which was characterised by age and occupation. I'd met people like Tom before, notably when I made a programme about Blue Streak, Britain's attempt to enter the space race. I don't know exactly what shaped them all, but they shared a character and resilience, a sense of duty which was ingrained in their DNA. The people who turned Blue Streak into what, from a technical standpoint, was the world's most successful rocket programme, were like charcters from a war-time film. They were principled, played by a very strict set of social rules, and were exceptionally good at what they did. Tom Tuohy was exactly that. As the interview progressed, I guided him through his story, and found it difficult to comprehend the courage he'd shown, and the casual way he had put his life at risk.

When the temperature in the reactor ran out of control during the annealing process, it was difficult to be sure what was going on. So Tom climbed more than four hundred feet to the top of the reactor chimney wearing breathing apparatus, and peered down to the Graphite far below. It was glowing red, and it was obvious that something was very wrong. Over the course of the next few hours he repeated the journey several times, and became increasingly alarmed as he saw the fire spread. Climbing to the top of the chimney in itself was quite some feat. I couldn't have managed it once. But Tom had done it wearing heavy breathing apparatus on each occasion. A number of different approaches were taken as the team battled to put out the fire, but what finally worked involved Tom risking his life in a most extraordinary move. He climbed up in front of the reactor face and used a scaffolding pole to push fuel rods out of the back and into a water channel. A dozen or so poles were connected up to hoses and inserted into the reactor about a foot above the channels at the heart of the fire. Tuohy ordered the water to be turned on and listened carefully for any signs of trouble. The fire was so hot, registering 1300° in places, that there was the danger of a Hydrogen explosion when the water contacted the hot metal of the fuel rods. It was risky, but the situation was now desperate, and there was a real chance that the biological shield around the reactor, designed to contain radiation, would be sufficiently weakened by the heat to cause it to collapse. However, it seemed that the water on its own was having little or no effect. So, in a final act, he had all cooling and ventilation fans turned off, hoping to starve the fire of oxygen. This combination finally began to work, and over the course of his next few inspections he saw the flames disappear and the glow begin to reduce. Tuohy's exposure to radiation would have been significant, but despite this, he lived until he was 90. The radiation released into the atmosphere spread across Europe, but although significant quantities of isotopes such as Iodine-131, Caesium-137 and Xenon-133 escaped, it could have been much worse had it not been for a part of the Pile chimney known as Cockcroft's Folly. And it was this that made our journey to the top of the Pile 2 chimney much more frightening.

Cockcroft's Follies were filter galleries, designed to contain the release of radiation in case of fire. Under normal circumstances such filters would be built at the bottom of the chimney for ease of construction and access for maintenance. But the Windscale filters weren't a part of the original plans. They were added after building work was under way in a decision which caused a great deal of acrimony at the time. But Cockcroft's insistence that the design be modified to include them was based upon a fortuitous misunderstanding.

There were two main nuclear sites in the United States which had been involved in manufacturing fissile material for the Manhattan Project. One was at Hanford in a remote part of Washington State. The other was at Oak Ridge, Tennessee. Hanford supplied the Plutonium-239 for the second bomb, dropped on Nagasaki, and Oak Ridge the Uranium-235 for the first bomb detonated on Hiroshima. Sir John Cockcroft was Director of the Atomic Energy Research Establishment, and he visited Oak Ridge shortly after a minor accident which involved a small release of radioactivity. At the time he was there, the belief was that the Clinton Reactor had been responsible for the release, and Cockcroft was impressed by the filter design which was thought to have caught many of the radioactive particles before they could escape into the atmosphere. He understood the significance of the filter in the event of an accident, and insisted that the Windscale Piles' design be modified accordingly. However, construction work had already begun, so the only place to build the galleries was at the top of the chimneys. And because the cross-section of the gallery was bigger than that of the chimney, it presented a problem for the hoist designer. As we stood at the bottom with our equipment waiting to ascend, something struck me as worrying. The chimney was actually quite a long way away. I didn't much like that.

Looking up, it all made sense. For the hoist to reach to the top, the track it climbed had to run vertically down from the edge of the filter gallery above, and since it was maybe thirty feet wider than the chimney, that's how far away we were standing. As if the idea that this strange looking contraption didn't seem to be attached to the chimney wasn't bad enough, I then turned my attention to the box we'd ride in. How should I put this? It didn't seem very robust. There was a cage type of door which should stop us falling out. There was a small window, perhaps eighteen inches square, in the wall on the right, and a small box on the floor below it. Otherwise, it seemed to be made from plywood, and I wasn't sure I wanted to trust my life to it. So I used a bit of psychology which I regularly resort to in these times of fear and stress. The people we were with had travelled in this thing before. They knew it. And they wouldn't get into it if it regularly fell out of the sky. So if they were willing to travel in it, there couldn't be anything to worry about. I had lectured myself in the same way when I was getting into the back seat of an RAF fast jet, and when I climbed rather awkwardly into the basket of a hot air balloon.

It always seemed to be when I got any distance from the ground that my problems started. I'm not a fan of heights. And neither is Eric. Our shared phobia worked well as a limiting factor on uncontrolled enthusiasm. My rule that I'd never ask someone to do something I wouldn't do myself set a sensible level for danger, and that was definitely A Good Thing. But despite that, here we were, about to get into this hoist and go a long way into the sky in a wooden box. Unfortunately, my limiting factor had been over-ruled. This was no longer about what we felt comfortable with. This was about saving face with the Sellafield press office. How could I play the part of the fearless, truth seeking journalist if I didn't have the courage to get into the box? So I took a breath, and walked forward.

I heard the cage door close behind me. Someone threw a switch and there was a jolt. The little box began to climb its way up its mast, and the ground slowly began to fall away. I became acutely aware that there was three-quarters of an inch of wood beneath my feet, the job of which was to prevent me from plunging to my death. To take my mind off this thought, to distract me from my inner harbingers of doom, I looked out of the window. I immediately released my mistake. Looking out of the window was a very bad idea. Just below the window was a very white face which belonged to Eric. He gave me a sort of grimace which spoke volumes. It empathised with the reaction he saw in me, and said "I'm not enjoying this either". It said "I wish you hadn't been so keen to accept the offer of a look at the top of the chimney". And it said "At least if anything goes wrong it'll be quick". My return look was much simpler. It said "How come you're sitting on the box so you're legs aren't shaking and you can't see out, while I'm stuck here looking out of the window?"

Finally, after what felt like several years of ageing, the little box jolted to a halt at the top. I breathed a sigh of relief. Now I could get out of this death-trap, but the thought was easier than the act. The cage door was slid back and I realised I was expected to get out. Only I had, once again, done the unthinkable. I'd looked down. And what I'd seen was possibly the most frightening image my eyes had ever captured. There was a gap between the edge of the box and the edge of the filter gallery. At most, it was three inches, and as a person who doesn't exactly have to run around in the shower to get wet there wasn't any chance I was going to slip through it. But by now all reason had been driven from my mind by the ascent to altitude, and I froze. After a second or two I felt a gentle nudge in the back. Eric was telling me that his fear of being in the hoist trumped my fear of getting out of it. So I stepped forward across the narrow void. Now that I was out of the little box and onto the solid mass of the chimney, things should have improved rapidly, but confusingly they didn't. There was the most amazing view of West Cumbria and the Irish Sea, and I could see the Isle of Man on the horizon. But I was observing the vista from 410 feet above where I was most comfortable, so I obeyed what my brain was telling me to do. I reached out and grabbed hold of a piece of scaffolding, and for the entire time I spent on top of that chimney I never once let go. I moved around a little, but I always maintained one point of contact. I don't know how he managed it, but Eric shot some pictures while we were up there. I was incapable of doing anything. My whole attention, to the exclusion of all else, was focused on maintaining a connection with the scaffolding. I don't know exactly how long we were up there, but my distress must have been very evident, because our hosts kindly suggested we get back to ground level.

I thought that was a wonderful idea until I was faced with getting back in the box. The three inch gap wasn't so much of a problem this time. It was more the thought of stepping off the chimney onto this three-quarter inch thick piece of wood between me and the 410 feet drop. I always try to take away a lesson from events like that one. This lesson was simple. Don't ever think of doing it again. And funnily enough, Eric promised to remind me if I forgot.

The meeting with Edward Teller provided me with inspiration for a programme within a science and technology series I was planning. The company's managing director, James Graham, fought a constant battle to keep the company vibrant and unique. Alongside the giants of the rest of the ITV network we were minnows, and he recognised we could be eaten up at any moment. His strategy was to focus on areas of programme making our larger cousins weren't involved with. He'd already turned his attention to religion and mountaineering, the latter because we covered an area which included the fells of the Lake District. I'd made several programmes about Sellafield by now, and he saw benefit in expanding the genre to include a more general coverage of science-related topics. It was a big step for the company, though more of an incremental step for me. I'd been gradually raising my game, becoming more adventurous in the standard of programmes I aimed for. As James and I sat in the canteen one lunchtime, he suggested I should put my interest in the subject to good use. I saw it as a green light to proceed, and set about coming up with half a dozen subjects to make programmes about. As I mentally cast around, my mind wandered back to the Hoover Tower at Stanford University, to a casual conversation with Teller after the interview was complete.

In the summer of 1950, Teller was walking to lunch at Los Alamos with Enrico Fermi and two other colleagues, Herbert York and Emil Konopinski. A few years later, it would be Konopinski's calculations which gave Teller confidence that a thermonuclear explosion would not set fire to the atmosphere and the oceans. As they made their way to eat at Fuller Lodge they discussed a spate of UFO sightings which had been making headlines. Austrian psychologist Carl Jung suggested there was something hard-wired in the human psyche which resonates with a belief in beings from other worlds. Indeed, as late as 1966 Carl Sagan, founder of the SETI programme, suggested that the moons of Mars might actually be artificial satellites. But on that day, the quartet argued about the possibility of journeying to other solar systems, travelling faster than the speed of light, and whether the UFO sightings could really be alien spacecraft. As they took their seats at a table, the conversation drifted off to other topics. Suddenly, Fermi said, "Don't you ever wonder where everybody is? If there are other beings in the universe," he reasoned, "why haven't they come to visit us?" The question became known as the Fermi Paradox. It was this subject that Teller raised as my crew packed away their equipment. And when I returned to relive the conversation in my mind, I realised what a worthy subject for exploration it was. It had a sound scientific base, but appealed to a huge range of people, and questioned the very roots of our existence. It fired my imagination, and I quickly realised it was a programme I had to make.

The filming took me to meet a collection of interesting and intelligent people. Among them was Glenn Campbell. He lived in a flat overlooking McCarran

Airport in Las Vegas, and was largely responsible for popularising interest in a US Air Force base at Groom Lake in Nevada, better known as Area 51. It was here, many argued, that the US government was storing and testing captured alien technology. I drove from Phoenix, Arizona to meet Glenn at his flat. The road north wasn't the fastest, and by the time I approached the Arizona/Nevada border at the Hoover Dam I realised we were going to be late. Today, there's a new bridge which carries Highway 93 high above the Colorado River below. But then, the only route across was by the narrow road over the dam itself, navigating hairpin bends down and up the steep walls of the canyon on either side. I stopped to phone ahead at a tourist shop on the Arizona side, parking at the vista point which offers such a dramatic view of the dam far below. When I apologised to Glenn, telling him where I was and that I was running half an hour behind schedule, I was confused by his response. "Judging from where you are," he said, "you're half an hour ahead of schedule, not behind." It turned out that I hadn't realised crossing the Hoover Dam also involved crossing a time zone. In Nevada, it was an hour earlier than in Arizona, and I was actually doing well in making my five o'clock appointment.

I'd been to Las Vegas a few times before, but it never fails to amaze me. On one early trip I drove direct from Oakland, California, across the bay from San Francisco. It was a circuitous route which circumnavigated the great obstacle of the Sierra Nevada mountains and took eleven hours. Eric sat next to me, a computer laptop balanced on his knee, its mapping software acquiring information from a GPS receiver stuck to the windscreen. I'd set Las Vegas as the destination point, and on the tick of every second the receiver would calculate how far we still had to go and display the distance on its tiny screen. But I-15's approach to the city takes a dog-leg, so it would only be when we arrived at the final turn that the distance displayed would be accurate. After what seemed like an eternity we finally arrived at the bend, and the road emerged from the mountains to begin the drop into to the Las Vegas bowl. By now it was pitch black, only the headlights of the car illuminating the world ahead. But then an astonishing thing happened. Suddenly, I felt as though I was being blinded by an intense light. It came from a huge television screen ahead on the Las Vegas strip. In the clear desert air I felt I could have reached out and touched it. It really seemed that close. I glanced at the GPS display and thought it must be faulty. According to the information it was presenting, the television was 19 miles away. I was so taken aback that the light should be so bright so far away that I took a mental note of the car's odometer reading, and sure enough, when we arrived at our destination we'd travelled a further 19 miles.

I remember reading that what's known as The Strip is not actually in Las Vegas. When the place began to be developed and the first casinos and hotels were built, there was a simple economic expedient to building outside the city. Taxes were lower. Modern Las Vegas began to be developed in the 1950s with the arrival of hotels such as The Sands and The Sahara. They were joined in 1957 by The Tropicana. I stayed there once, and was fascinated by what I found while wandering the corridors. Adorning the walls were beautiful old photographs of the site from not long after its opening. The area looked very different then, with an open vista across The Strip where New York, New York now stands. As I padded along on the thick carpet, marvelling at the quality of these old prints, each having captured its own unique part of history, I stopped dead in my tracks, unable to believe what I was seeing. The foreground of one photograph showed the frontage of The Tropicana. But what I'd seen, what had grabbed my attention so much, what stood high on the horizon, was a large, tall, white mushroom cloud, the unmistakeable signature of a nuclear explosion. It was proof, if it were needed, of the proximity of the Nevada Test Site to the north. I should have paid closer attention to that image.

I navigated to Glenn Campbell's flat, and he met us at the foot of the stairs to his front door. He explained that the unmarked Boeing 737s which ferry workers to Area 51 each day were about to arrive, and suggested we'd get some good shots from his doorway. He was right, and once the workers had dispersed we went inside. The first thing he said was a plea to be as quiet as possible. His downstairs neighbour worked nights, and slept during the day. No sooner had I acknowledged this than the sound recordist dropped one of our lights with a resounding bang. He was suitably embarrassed, as was I. Before I began the interview, Glenn asked me something odd. What did I want him to say? I explained that I wasn't going to put words in his mouth, but he didn't seem satisfied. So he put it another way. "I'm not going to tell you there are aliens at Groom Lake," he said. I laughed, and assured him that the programme I was making was a serious documentary, and I didn't want him to invent stories about little green men to appease me. Now we understood each other, things went well. I was pleased I was dealing with someone who had a sensible approach to this part of the tale I was making, and I decided that he was a smart guy who had found a way to make a few dollars from the same intrinsic fascination with the idea of alien life that had led to my conversation with Teller. Campbell spoke of how the existence of Area 51 was like a Rorschach ink blot from which everyone could infer their own meaning.

Afterwards, he told me how to get as close to Groom Lake as possible without getting arrested or shot. It triggered another hard-wired reaction in me which is characterised in American road films, the romance and excitement of a long and adventurous road trip, with just a hint of danger. After a night in Vegas, we set off the following morning in search of the pot of gold at the end of the rainbow. I headed north-east out of Las Vegas on I-15, past Nellis Air Force Base, the parent of Groom Lake. After a short while I turned north onto Highway 93, the road which had brought us to Las Vegas from Phoenix. In the first 60 miles I encountered just two bends of any significance, and we barrelled along across a desert landscape that was truly awesome. But then we encountered something which caused a dramatic change in our surroundings. Water. Now there was touch of greenery on either side of the road in a ribbon no more than a mile wide, and as we approached the small settlement of Alamo we passed two bodies of water, the Lower and Upper Pahranagat Lakes. The names of two other collections of houses gave a clue to the source of this giver of life, Ash Springs and Crystal Springs. I took the opportunity to fill the fuel tank at the only petrol station I'd see for hours. It was a wise decision. And then at Crystal Springs I swung left onto Highway 375, a green sign proudly proclaiming it to be the Extraterrestrial Highway.

375 initially struck out to the south-west until it cleared a small ridge. Then it turned north-west, and we travelled 16 miles straight as an arrow across the high desert. When we left Las Vegas we'd been at an altitude of two thousand feet. Shortly, we'd pass five and a half thousand. At the end of this long straight, the road again wriggled across a small ridge, and as we emerged onto the next section of flat desert, the dirt track road I was searching for appeared on the left. Again, the desert air distorted the distance. This track slowly descended into a shallow valley before climbing the far side and disappearing between some low mounds. I left the tarmac and bumped down onto the surface of the desert to begin the drive of few hundred yards to the mounds. But as I drove, the perspective seemed

to stretch, and the little clump of hills came no closer. We passed by individual Joshua Trees, so named by Mormon settlers who passed through here in the 19th century. By the time we reached the point where the road disappeared from view we'd travelled, not a few hundred yards, but four miles. I was learning that this desert could easily confuse the mind, and turn out to be a dangerous place. But ahead, those dangers were much more overt. The road disappeared through a low pass before dropping down into a small bowl. There was a pair of ominous signs, and a yellow line painted across the track.

I pulled into a small parking area carved into the desert surface by a constant stream of visiting cars, and climbed out of the air conditioned atmosphere of the vehicle into the brutal desert heat. I read one of the signs which warned that photography was prohibited. Oh well. That was one law we were about to break. The other advised me that the use of deadly force was authorised. I thought that getting shot might cast a shadow on the day, so I made very sure the crew knew exactly where the boundary of the restricted area lay, and advised them to take the fuse out of their sense of humour for the moment and stay on the right side of it. Glenn Campbell had told me what to expect. We'd passed over sensors under the track which reported our presence to the guard hut hidden around the next corner. On the hillside above I saw at least two cameras peering down at us, and could only imagine the guards sitting watching, imploring us to cross the line so they could come and get us. Up to the right, perhaps half a mile away, was a four-wheel drive vehicle, parked so its occupants had a clear view of the approach road. I realised that they must have been able to see the dust trail we'd been creating since we left the highway. These were what Campbell had referred to as the Cammo Dudes, private contractors employed to keep away tourists like us. And what I had to keep in mind was that they had guns and we didn't. This was still the Wild West, and the best we could do would be to avoid attracting too much attention. So we got the filming done as quickly as possible, and in the tradition of all westerns, high-tailed it out of town. Or actually into town. The town of Rachel, Nevada.

I say town, but it wasn't like any town you'd recognise. There were barely more than a dozen properties, but two of them stood out from the rest. The first was the grandly named Area 51 Research Center, a bright yellow wooden structure, the architecture of which appeared closely related to the sort of houses you'd find in a trailer park. The other was The Little A'Le'Inn, a bar, restaurant and motel. The purpose of both was to cash in on the steady stream of believers who made the same trek we had. I was aware there was bad blood between the two businesses, so by the time we headed for a burger we had assumed the persona of tourists who'd just travelled for two hours from Las Vegas to visit a two horse town when one of them had gone on holiday. We seemed to get away with it.

A few years later I found myself back in Rachel. I revisited in the company of a friend from the Isle of Man,
in a one-week Boy's Outing which explored some of my
favourite haunts in the western United States. Steve had
an enthusiasm for UFO theories, and was particularly
keen to see Area 51. At the bright yellow wooden
research centre, I asked the occupier how he'd ended
up there. On my previous visit, the store had been run
by Glenn Campbell's girl-friend. This time it turned out
to be a bloke from Oregon. He'd bought the business
from Campbell, who probably thought the UFO thing
had run its course. As we chatted, I asked him about
local abandoned towns from the era of the Gold Rush.
The idea of wandering through a piece of real history
intrigued me. He said most of them were a distance
further north, but pointed me in the direction of an
old silver mine about nine miles south of town. After
another excellent burger from The Little A'Le'Inn we
set off to find it. I turned off 375 at the appointed place,
and once again found myself on a dirt track heading
into the mountains. I drove as far as I could before
the track became too rough for further progress. As
with the Area 51 track, there was a parking spot which
had been worn down by visitors. I locked the car and
we continued on foot. It was hard going climbing the
steep track up the canyon, not helped by the thinner
atmosphere at this altitude. It was such a beautiful day,
with a clear blue sky and visibility that stretched to last
week. I'd become wary of estimating distances in the
desert by now, but the snow covered mountains to the
north shone bright from perhaps a hundred miles away.

As we climbed, we passed the snow line. But it was warm and pleasant, and I was enjoying the experience. The track steepened, and the altitude and the burger began to take a toll on my energy and enthusiasm. I decided that we'd have a look around the next corner, and if we found nothing we'd turn back. Fortune favoured us that day, because as we rounded the bend in the path I saw an old, rusted cart on the hill above, with a trail of spoil leading down towards us. We climbed a bit more until we were level with the cart, then turned back towards it along an access track. It revealed itself as belonging to the mine, and sat on the remains of a narrow-gauge railway that led towards a shaft which disappeared into the mountain. We approached the entrance and peered inside.

The contrast between the darkness of the shaft and the bright Nevada sunshine prevented us from seeing much, so I stepped in through the portal. As the light dimmed a bit, my eyes adjusted to the change in brightness and I was able to see a little better. My main concern was disturbing a bear. Did they live around here? Then I saw a wooden door on the left, with a painted sign on it which read "Danger. Explosives." Back in Rachel we'd been told about an old-timer who'd lived in a shack way out in the desert. Someone had gone to visit him to help tidy up the house. When they looked under the floor they discovered, with some measure of alarm, a box of dynamite. It was very old, and a long time previously the nitro-glycerine had started to weep from the adsorbent. In such a state it was highly susceptible to exploding with the slightest shock. So I decided to ignore the door, and cautiously walked forward into the darkness. I really wished I'd brought a torch with me, but my Boy Scout instincts aren't highly developed. Eventually, perhaps thirty yards in, I had to give up. No matter how hard I tried I just couldn't see anything in the darkness ahead, and I was pretty sure that bears had good night vision. So we turned around and headed back towards the safety of the daylight.

Back at the car, I headed for the long dirt track road that I knew led to the back gate of Area 51. Steve's excitement grew with every passing mile. This was what he'd waited so long to see, having devoured the programme I'd made after coming here. This was to be the highlight of his holiday. We drove along the four mile track to the warning signs, and his trip was instantly complete. He stood, drinking in the moment before we took the obligatory, illegal photographs.

With heavy hearts we got back in the car and turned around, Las Vegas and the hotel two long hours away. On the drive back to Highway 93 we stopped amongst the Joshua Trees and Steve decided he wanted to take home a souvenir of this important day in his life. He scanned the desert floor looking for something suitable, and a few feet away his eyes came to rest on a rock that was different from any others around. It was small, maybe four or five inches across, jet black, but glass-like with a faceted, highly polished surface. He cheerfully picked it up and popped it into his rucksack.

Sometime after our return home Steve called me from the Isle of Man. He told me an odd thing had happened. He'd decided that his souvenir, which he inventively called Rock, deserved pride of place in his back garden. So it was placed in the centre of the grass in homage to his seminal moment in Nevada. But as time went by Steve noticed a change. Slowly but surely the grass within eighteen inches of Rock withered and died. There was now, he said, a brown circle in the middle of his garden with the black, glass-like souvenir at its centre. We joked about what could have caused this bizarre effect, and our lives moved on.

Rock came back into focus when I was filming a couple of years later. The landmark series examined the history of Mankind's control of the atom. Amongst the many places I visited in the course of filming was the National Radiological Protection Board, a public body which carried out research into the effects of radiation. As was usual, once the interview was over I was able to have a more relaxed chat with the interviewee.

I don't know what brought Rock to mind, but I related the story of Steve and his dying grass, and described the black glass-like souvenir he'd brought home. "Do you know," I asked, "what it could be?" "Oh yes," came the reply. "It's Trinitite." Everything dropped into place like a Kaleidoscope of images falling in front of my eyes. The photograph on the wall in the Tropicana Hotel. The inspiring chat with Edward Teller. A photograph of The Gadget atop its tower before the Trinity Test.

My interviewee explained that the heat from a nuclear blast was so great that it fused sand into glass, and captured within it was radiation from the bomb. The rock Steve took home, the scientist explained, had been the product of a nuclear explosion.

A little while after this revelation, Steve left the Isle of Man to start a new and exciting life in Canada. Just as I had been inspired by Teller, our trip to the United States had inspired him. He graciously and unselfishly left Rock behind, and presumably it still lies somewhere in the back garden of his old house in the south of the island as a monument to his curiosity. And that's the story, until now untold, of how the Isle of Man became a secret repository for a tiny piece of nuclear history, plucked by an innocent from close to the Nevada Test Site, and carried a third of the way around the world to a new resting place in a Manx housing estate.

As far as I'm aware, no plaque marks the spot. There's no Henry Moore sculpture. Just a small circle of dead grass.

FLIGHTS OF FANCY

It was the Chinese philosopher Lao Tzu who opined *Even the longest journey begins with the first step*. I feel an affinity with the 6th century BC record keeper at the Zhou dynasty court. We both arrived at the same conclusion through independent thinking. I only wish I could claim to be blessed with the great man's wisdom, but sadly any such foolish assertion would surely fall at the first hurdle. Lao Tzu wrote the Tao de Ching, or The Tao as it is often called. Tao means The Way, and I suppose it could be described as a guide to the workings of the Universe. One of the key themes of these teachings is wuwei, or doing nothing. It sounds a little odd at first hearing, the concept that you can achieve something by doing nothing. But I discovered, without having previously known of the record keeper, that I was using his teachings in my approach to programme making.

When I began my career at the BBC I was heavily influenced by a report on the Corporation's workings by Lord Annan. He had heaped criticism on producers who lived in ivory towers, oblivious to the reality of life in the outside world. This influence helped me create my own way of working, and led to the idea that my programmes should act as a lens on the world rather than a filter. While many of my colleagues intricately planned their news reports or programmes from their desk before going out to fit reality to their pre-conceptions, I preferred to start off with nothing more than an outline plan, waiting to see what the world would throw at me and reacting accordingly. Lao Tzu's wuwei worked well with that approach. Do nothing. Delay making decisions about the value of the various elements until everything, almost magically, comes together. It could be an intense experience. A series of Innovators, my science and technology programme, covered half a dozen very different subjects, ranging from the workings of the human brain to the search for extra-terrestrial intelligence, and involved in-depth interviews with more than seventy world-class experts from around the globe. Holding these interviews in my head for six or seven months, along with the images we'd shot to accompany them, was a challenge, but it meant I could arrive at a balanced view of the topic, and understand the relative importance of what each expert had to say.

If Lao Tzu's journey began with the first step, mine would often start in a more modern way by boarding an aeroplane. My most regular destination in the early days would be the Isle of Man, and we'd set off around

5 am for the drive to Blackpool Airport to catch the first flight of the day. It was a very personal service on a small Twin Otter aircraft, the ugly duckling of the airline industry, which carried fewer than twenty passengers. I was learning to fly at the time, and always felt this charming little aeroplane was not too far removed from what I was used to in my weekly lessons.

Two companies competed on the route between Blackpool and the Isle of Man, both using the same aircraft type. I usually flew with Spacegrand, a tiny start-up which eventually grew into one of Europe's biggest regional carriers, FlyBE. There was a supreme friendliness about the operation, and a perk which would be unthinkable in today's aviation world. I'd always try to make sure I was first on board, because Spacegrand would allow one of the passengers to sit in the co-pilot's seat next to the captain. It gave me the opportunity to learn more about a job I had an interest in from the point of view of a happy amateur, and the pilot would chat with me and answer my questions on the journey across the Irish Sea. On one occasion, travelling back to Blackpool in poor weather with the cloud base hovering around 200 feet, I was excited to be given the task of watching for the runway lights while the pilot concentrated on flying the instrument approach.

This cosy arrangement was one I enjoyed and took for granted, but on one particular flight it led to a slightly embarrassing situation. On this occasion we were flying with the competitor airline, and it must have been the first time I'd used them. As had become the norm, I almost sprinted across the tarmac of the apron to be first on board, and made my way forward to what I viewed by now as my seat. As I plonked myself into place I attracted a look of disdain and alarm from the pilot. "What do you think you're doing?" he asked. "You can't sit there." I was a little taken aback, but explained that the other airline carried a passenger in this seat on their flights. In the sort of condescending voice he must have perfected at flight school he told me, "Well we're a professional airline. You'll have to move." I slunk back to a seat in the cabin, thankful that my dash for the aircraft meant that few had yet boarded behind me to watch my ignominious departure.

The Twin Otter was snug, with a pair of seats down one side of the aisle and rows of single seats down the other. There wasn't a huge amount of space for legs and knees, and on one particular trip this proved to be the undoing of one unfortunate traveller. I had been co-opted onto a production about the Isle of Man which was to be presented by Melvyn Bragg, largely because I knew the people on the island who could get things done if we ran into problems. The travel day saw some terrible weather moving across the Irish Sea, and I knew we'd be in for a rough ride. The crossing from Blackpool only took half an hour or so, but for some members of the team this would be a long, memorable and miserable time. I sat with the sound recordist, Cliff, wedged together in a pair of tiny seats, with belts tightly fastened. Cliff had been an RAF officer, and his flying experience meant I would often seek him out for advice while I was learning to fly. The Twin Otter is an unpressurised aircraft, so its operating altitude is normally limited to 10,000 feet, but for the hop across the water we'd likely be no higher than around half that. It was raining heavily, the wind was blowing strongly, and we were heading towards a band of thunderstorms. But Cliff and I sat there cheerfully waiting for whatever the weather gods would throw at us.

If we were expecting the worst, we weren't disappointed. On the way to the island, conditions deteriorated. There wasn't any point in looking outside. There was just a dark grey, almost black mass of angry cloud out there, with a stream of water cascading down the window. Inside, the view wasn't much better. I saw the white, worried faces of a group of people who might have been straight out of Central Casting. If you wanted characters for a disaster movie, they were all here, gearing themselves up for the audition. There was a nun, a senior couple going on holiday, and the parents and two children who constantly sang "We're all going on a summer holiday" to take their mind off the turbulence. Each was secretly praying that the laws of physics wouldn't be disproved today, and that our little flying machine would suddenly break out of the clouds to be bathed in warm, reassuring sunshine with the green fields of Shangri-la below. The only people I couldn't spot were the man with the guitar, and a guy with a box in his lap containing a beating heart for a transplant.

Dispersed amongst these would-be actors were the members of our film crew, and they looked equally unhappy. The production assistant was showing off her screaming talents each time the aircraft was tossed around the sky by a giant hand. She was very impressive. The director was a deathly white, subtly tinged with green, looking as though the cameraman had forgotten to carry out a white balance to correct his skin tones. And as Cliff and I sipped our drinks - curiously, no-one else had ordered anything - we watched the row in front of us with growing fascination. Another crew member sat there, rigid with fear. A crimson tide was slowly rising up his neck, and small beads of sweat began to trickle in the opposite direction. We glanced at each other, an unspoken communication signalling that we knew what lay in store, grateful that we were behind our colleague rather than ahead of him. Suddenly, it came. With a noise loud enough to cause alarm throughout the aircraft, he vomited violently. In itself, this was bad enough. But, as in the last milliseconds of a road accident, the world switched to slow motion. It was as if we were weightless in space, the large volume of regurgitated breakfast clumping together as it moved forward in a graceful parabola. At the Vomiting Olympics it would have attracted a score of at least 9.5. And then, just as its forward energy was spent, the world snapped back to real time, and we watched it flop into the anorak hood of the man in the next row forward. There followed the silence of anticlimax, broken only by another Oscar-winning scream from the PA. And then I began to giggle. It was that infectious giggle that's impossible to restrain, as when Mary Tyler-Moore started laughing during the funeral service of Chuckles the Clown. In her case it was the memory of Chuckles' catch-phrase which set her off. "*A little song. A little dance. A little seltzer down your pants.*" In mine, it was the images which formed in my brain, anticipating events upon arrival on the Isle of Man. I could see the unfortunate man in the anorak alighting from the aircraft and making the dash across a hundred yards of tarmac to the terminal through the pouring rain, reaching behind his head to yank up his anorak hood for protection. The giggle became a roar, and soon Cliff was joining in, unsure of the exact reasons for the laughter, but happy to become a part of the moment, savouring the emotional release on an otherwise joyless journey.

The flights to the Isle of Man were normally a part of the pleasurable experience of going there. They created a sense of adventure in what was otherwise a long, mind-numbing journey. I can still remember the act of a comedian friend, Dave Wolfe, when he related the tale of his flight. "I flew across here on Manx Airlines," he said. "Tiny little aeroplane. When we were all on board, they took away the steps at the back and it tipped over. Before we took off, the stewardess came round with sweets for your ears. I didn't half look a prat. But it was a nice flight. We stopped at Southport on the way to do some crop spraying. When we were half way across the pilot came back and said, 'Has anyone been to the Isle of Man before? Is it kidney-shaped?' Still, we made a very good landing, quite near the airport." I'm not sure why I remember it so well, though it may have something to do with hearing the same performance, word for word, at a different charity event I was filming a few weeks later. And who was sitting in the audience laughing at the jokes? None other than Dave Wolfe. It seems that the act was shared amongst a group of comedians for the times they worked on the charity circuit.

The route to the Isle of Man was circuitous for us. We'd drive from Carlisle to Blackpool to catch the flight, and although we were only in the air for thirty minutes or so, the entire journey could take three hours. Blackpool was the least inconvenient of the airports for us to use, but we were occasionally forced to go further afield if the flight I wanted to catch was full. My rule for travelling has always been to use the smallest available airport, which usually means the smallest available aircraft. By keeping things to a minimum, everything seemed quicker and more personal. This was brought home to me on one occasion when there were no seats available from the seaside airport, and I was forced to book the trip on a larger aircraft from Manchester.

There were four problems with flying from Manchester. It was further away, parking was more challenging, the terminal was huge by comparison, and the roads were a lot busier. We'd all collaborated over the calculation of how long it would take to get to Manchester Airport, and we were all rather too optimistic for comfort. As we crawled along the final section of motorway, I could see aircraft taking off and landing in the distance, and kept glancing anxiously at my watch. I hated being late for anything, and the consequences of turning up even a few minutes after the check-in closed would be disastrous. When, finally, the slow-moving lines of traffic completely clogged the road, we came to a standstill and my heart sank. Time took on the consistency of treacle and my heart rate soared. But eventually we arrived at the terminal, and there was a frantic dash for trolleys to carry our equipment and cases, and then to park the vehicle. I always made a special effort to be nice to the check-in staff, firstly because they had to deal with a lot of stressed people every day and I felt that a smile and a kind word would help relieve some of the pressure, and secondly because it sometimes helped me with any inadvertent minor transgressions.

Once, at the tiny Bakersfield Airport on the edge of the Mojave Desert, we were checking in for a commuter flight down to LAX, the massive international hub at Los Angeles. The check-in agent did everything from inspecting our tickets to baggage handling. He looked like he was straight out of college, and from his physique I guessed he'd played American football. But I noticed that he wore a leather support which offered protection for his back, and as he reached for one of the large, heavy equipment cases I warned him to take care because it was heavy. A red line on the display of the huge scales behind the counter showed the weight limit, and as he put the aluminium box down the pointer soared past it. He glanced up at me and smiled. "Bang on!" he said. I smiled back a thanks as he lifted the box back off the scales and reached for a second one. Between the three of us there were fourteen bags and boxes, and avoiding excess baggage charges was a constant battle on the see-saw of life, overcoming rules and regulations, on one side with charm and on the other with the judicious use of humour. But sometimes, there'd be a trip hazard that got in the way and produced the need for a bit of extra finessing. I hated it when it was caused by the carelessness of one of my colleagues. Allan was only following my lead in trying to be helpful to the agent, but having already seen the pointer sail past the red line, his words could have been more considered. The agent picked up the second box and hefted it in his hand. "This one feels about the same," he said as he by-passed the scales. Lifting bags day in and day out had given him an internal measure, and he knew this box was no light weight. "Watch out," warned Allan. "That one's heavier." I met the agent's eyes again, a slightly embarrassed look on my face as he decided whether to continue his charade. "Oh, it's good," he replied with a wink as I kicked Allan hard on the ankle.

However, no amount of jollying on my part could soften the stern reaction from the agent at Manchester as we rushed to the desk that morning, pushing two trolleys stacked with equipment and luggage. I could see her eyes take in the sight before her, and she was not pleased. I switched on my apologetic mode, but it made little difference. "You'll have to run," she said as she passed us our boarding cards. A few breathless, sweaty minutes later we were walking across the tarmac towards the aircraft. This one was about twice the size of the one on the Blackpool route, a 36 seat Shorts 360 built in Belfast. It wasn't what you could call pretty, and was referred to in the airline industry as The Shed, largely because that's what it looked like. Passengers, I discovered, were known as SLC - Self Loading Cargo. Once we'd self-loaded ourselves onto the last row of seats we sat there, grateful we'd actually made it. Now it was someone else's job to drive the final sector of our journey.

I began to look forward to a coffee on the way, and became aware of a lot of banging behind us. I'd later discover that the ground crew were unloading the cargo they'd previously put in the hold to make way for our collection of bags and boxes. The flight attendant floated by and I smiled at her, an innocent and naive question forming on my lips. I was thinking ahead to the first of the interviews I'd arranged on the island, wondering if we'd make it on time. "Are we going to be delayed?" I asked. She turned with the snarl of a pit bull terrier. "Yes," she snapped. "Because eleven of you were late!" She flounced off down the aisle, and I began to re-evaluate the idea of coffee. I didn't relish the prospect of it accidentally ending up in my lap.

One of my colleagues was faced with flying from Leeds/Bradford Airport when he left it very late before trying to book. Getting there was a marathon cross-country journey along narrow, winding roads. But he needn't have worried. The cameraman due to go with him didn't like flying, so he complained that the mental stress of starting the journey by travelling for several hours in the wrong direction would be too much for him. He actually got away with it, and they all eventually travelled by ferry instead. The result of that smart move meant it took a day to get there, and he got to sit at the bar for four hours on the way across.

There were occasions when I managed a more direct route. The Isle of Man's Ronaldsway Airport was less than a hundred miles from Carlisle, and although there were no commercial flights available, there were some occasions when the convenience of chartering made life much easier. There were two when it was an absolute necessity.

I was in the newsroom early, preparing for a trip to the island to meet Douglas Hurd, the British Home Secretary. He was travelling from London to meet with the island's Chief Minister, Miles Walker, for what were described as constitutional talks. A press conference was being held late afternoon and I'd be there to ask Douglas some suitably pertinent questions. I was looking forward to a leisurely drive to Blackpool to have some fish and chips on the prom ahead of the lunchtime flight. But my plans were changed in an instant by a phone call. The newsroom was still sparsely populated when the phone rang, so I picked up the call and discovered I was talking with someone from ITN, the news arm of ITV. "We'd like some reaction from the Home Secretary to the Belgian prison riots overnight," the voice on the other end said. "He's on a flight to the Isle of Man, arriving at 10:30. Can you get someone to meet him there and interview him?" For The Voice it was doubtless a simple request, but the practicality of being a hundred miles away across the water less than two hours later was a logistical nightmare. But, of course, I said yes. I immediately put a call in to Air Traffic Control at Carlisle Airport. I was learning to fly at the time, and knew the controllers well. "Is anyone going west this morning?" I asked. It seemed that the owner of a helicopter flying school was headed to Belfast in his twin-engined aeroplane, so I called him to ask if he would go via the Isle of Man. "Of course," he replied. "But you need to get here now."

The Heysel Stadium disaster had occurred two years previously, in 1985, at the European Cup final between Liverpool and Juventus. Thirty nine people died during the violence, and the resultant police investigation led to the extradition of twenty-six people charged with manslaughter. There was a perception amongst Belgian prisoners that the British were being given preferential treatment, and rioting broke out in protest. It was this that ITN wanted a reaction to.

We bundled equipment and cases into the crew vehicle and set off for the airport at speed. Our pilot was anxious to get going and was waiting for us at the aircraft when we arrived. Within a few minutes we were taxying to the runway. The weather was excellent, with blue skies and a few scattered clouds high above us. We hadn't been in the air for long before I got my first glimpse of the island. The dark smudge on the horizon gradually resolved into the peak of Snaefell, the mountain which stands majestically overlooking the northern plain. The water crossing took no more than twenty minutes, and we began descending effortlessly through the calm air of the morning, with the airport's runway just a few miles ahead.

The landing was uneventful, and we were soon unloading our equipment and preparing to film. As I stood on the east apron in the sunshine, my view of the west apron was obscured by the long covered corridor which led from the terminal building to the departure gates. On our side it was deserted and calm, but I would soon discover that the west apron was a different world entirely. I looked to my left and saw a jet flaring to land on the runway we'd been on ourselves just a few minutes previously. It was the Manx Airlines BAC 1-11 from London Heathrow, and somewhere on board was Douglas Hurd. I urged the crew into action, and with a quick call of thanks to our pilot I set off at a trot towards a door into the corridor.

I pulled it open, took three paces across the passageway, and opened the door on the opposite side. As I stepped back into the sunshine I quickly scanned the view, beginning to take in the challenges facing me. The first was a Special Branch officer who looked round to see who these uninvited guests were. If we'd been anywhere else we'd probably have been arrested there and then. To be fair, we had an advantage because we'd arrived in our own aircraft. That meant we were already airside, and I hadn't had to find a way of getting through security. But nevertheless we had no accreditation, and there was undoubtedly a very long list of rules we were breaking by being there. But this was the Isle of Man. "Hi Ian," he said with a smile, and made no effort to stop our progress. By now the big jet had arrived on the apron, and I knew that the Home Secretary would be first off. The cameraman was already filming, and I needed a plan to get my interview.

There was quite a delegation waiting. At the head of the line I could see the island's Lieutenant Governor, Major General Sir Laurence New, with his ADC. Next to them was Chief Minister Miles Walker, followed by the rest of his cabinet. I knew that I had one shot at this. If I missed out, the Home Secretary would be whisked away from my reach in the motorcade. So I did the only thing I could think of. I sauntered innocently across and stood on the end of the line of dignitaries waiting for their hand shake. Nobody seemed to pay much attention to me. Most of them knew me, and I was just accepted as part of the landscape. Douglas Hurd made his way down the line of important people until he reached the unimportant one at the end. For an instant there was a look of puzzlement in his eyes until I introduced myself and asked him for his reaction to the prison riots in Belgium. He was an impeccable performer, and immediately gave a polished response. Within a couple of minutes the interview was over and he went on his way. I made a bee-line for Michael Woods, the Governor's ADC, and asked him to apologise for my having gate-crashed the party. Michael was gracious as always, and assured me I hadn't caused any offence.

In those days we were still shooting on film. Electronic news gathering was a few years away yet. An added complication was that we were the only ITV company to use Agfa film. Everyone else shot on Kodak. The chemical process for each was different, which meant that no-one else could process the film we'd just shot. So I worked on hiring an aircraft to take the film to Carlisle, while the cameraman transferred it from the camera's magazine to a film can. Before long our work was done. The film was on its way, and our next job was the press conference we'd originally been travelling to the island to cover. But that wasn't until five o'clock, several hours away. So we headed to our hotel to check in, and before long were firmly ensconced in seats in the bar.

The Palace Hotel's Round Bar was run by Lil, a lovely lady of uncertain age. Rumour had it that she managed to mislead management for years so that she could avoid having to retire. Certainly, the place was never the same after she left. The bar, as the name suggested, was round and occupied a spot in the middle of the large room. There was a slightly raised area by the wall-to-ceiling windows which gave an unobstructed view of the beach and Douglas Bay. My favourite table was in the corner nearest the door, and from there I could watch the new arrivals as they made their way towards Lil for their favourite tipple. The Round Bar was a place of happy memories, and for a few years was one of the places to be seen. This meant that I could meet and entertain many of the top people on the island without having to stray far from my seat. It was also a place where there was much laughter - invariably from my corner.

During one visit, the manager approached me at breakfast. David was a softly spoken Scot who'd shared a drink with me on more than a few occasions, and we'd become good friends. The local branch of the Round Table was having its monthly lunch at the hotel that day, and he wanted me to know that Hugh Williams, head of the BBC in Manchester, would be addressing them. He provided the information with a small smile, knowing that it would bring out my inner Dennis the Menace. I smiled back and said thanks for the heads-up. I was working with an unusual crew on that trip. Both had come from the studio, and although the studio cameramen liked to think they were the same - some imagined better - than those who worked on the road, in reality they struggled to cope with a real world environment. In the studio everything was carefully controlled. In the outside world things would happen without warning. I called this News. They called it Frightening. The alarm bells had begun to ring when we checked in at the airport. Whilst the cameraman and I produced small cases with our overnight toiletries and clothes, the sound recordist handed over a Tesco carrier bag containing his. But there was no doubting their enthusiasm. Unlike some of the others who had earned a degree in being sullen, they were like eager puppies, excited at the prospect of exploring somewhere new.

I gathered them together and explained that we would have to work faster than normal that morning. I wanted to be back at the hotel by midday. Under normal circumstances a news crew would do two stories a day. On the Isle of Man I'd sometimes manage nine. But this morning was relatively quiet. Our first call would be at a new satellite ground station which had been built by Manx Telecom, and then we were off to interview the Chief Minister at Government Buildings. On the way to the new satellite dish I put in a call to the Chief Minister's secretary to ask if we could come half an hour early, and she readily agreed.

The satellite ground station was very new indeed, and although the electronics had all been commissioned and were working, the land around the dish was still a sea of mud. Neither Manx Telecom's Managing Director nor I were enthralled by the prospect of trekking through the quagmire, so the interview was safely conducted on a tarmac path which circled the facility. But afterwards, Jim the cameraman - remember the puppy-like eagerness - donned his rugged walking boots so he could get nearer for a good selection of pictures. Before long, I was looking anxiously at my watch and urging a return to the car. We were getting dangerously close to the time of our appointment with the Chief Minister, and having brought the interview forward, I didn't want to be late. Eventually, Jim heeded my pleas, and we piled back into the vehicle and sped off towards Government Buildings. Luck was on our side that day. There's a small parking bay outside the island's seat of government, and a car-sized space was waiting for us.

It was here that the crew's lack of experience was exposed. Studios tend not to have thick mud on the floor, so Jim had presumably never had to deal with muddy boots on an assignment before. And his were certainly the muddiest I had ever seen. The full height of each boot was caked with a brown oozing mess, at least an inch thick. Most people would simply have taken them off and put their shoes back on, but the collection of neurons in Jim's brain which fired didn't consider that solution, and this would ultimately lead to trouble. As he got out of the car, he spotted a window cleaner hard at work on the enormous area of glass at the front of the building, and an idea formed in his head. He approached the man with the chamois and said, "We're going to see the Chief Minister. Could I borrow your bucket?" The hapless window cleaner didn't know what to say in response to the decidedly odd request, but obediently stood back. Jim took a pace forward and plunged a boot into the soapy water. I groaned inwardly, and suddenly decided I didn't want to be a part of this scene. So, after giving directions to the office, I left the pair to resolve the argument between the filthy footwear and the soapy water. I headed for the lift, quietly humming George Formby's song *The Window Cleaner*, aware that a statue of the singer stood just a few hundred yards away in Ridgeway Street, commemorating his 1935 film *No Limit* in which he wins the Isle of Man TT.

I took the lift to the top floor, and headed for the Chief Minster's office. It was in the opposite corner from the lift, so I had to walk along two sides of the building to get there. In doing so, I crossed into the precincts of Tynwald, the Manx Parliament, and the quality of the deep blue carpet reflected the importance of where I was. The Chief Minister's secretary greeted me and showed me into his office. Miles Walker had been a Member of the House of Keys since 1976 and was appointed Chief Minister the previous year. I knew him well and he greeted me warmly. I explained that the crew were just behind me and thanked him for seeing me early. We sat and discussed the subject of the interview, and within five minutes or so the cameraman and sound recordist arrived.

Sometimes, what appears on the television screen can look very natural, when the situation in reality is anything but. There was a painting on the wall behind Miles' desk which was at an awkward height, and I asked Jim to set up the camera low on the tripod so that it would be looking up at the Chief Minister. This meant that the painting would fit naturally into the framing of the shot. But it also meant that, to appear normal, the Chief Minister would have to be looking down to the level of the lens. That, in turn, meant I had to crouch rather uncomfortably on the floor.

This technique was indelibly etched into my brain by an incident at Ronaldsway Airport a few years earlier. During TT Week, there was always a series of aerobatic displays by a collection of different aircraft. The Red Arrows were regulars, and this particular year Brian Lecomber was also there with his Pitts Special. I'd first met Brian when I worked in radio, and had interviewed him when his excellent book, *Talk Down*, was published. He was a highly skilled pilot, and his displays involved manoeuvres I didn't think aircraft were capable of. We'd already filmed his display, and I wanted an interview to go with it. Without giving much thought to it, we'd set things up with Brian standing on a tarmac path and the camera on its tripod on the grass alongside. The grassy area was perhaps six inches higher than the tarmac, and Brian, who wasn't the tallest of people, was looking perplexed as he gazed up at the lens. "You won't make me look small, will you?" he asked my cameraman, Eric. "No. Of course not," said Eric. "What I'll do is lower the height of the tripod so that the lens is at eye level with you, and no-one will know what height you are." Brian looked satisfied by this. But rather than leave it alone, the electrician decided to add his helpful two-pence worth. "Yes," he said. "It's a trick they used in Hollywood with Alan Ladd. He was a midget too."

There followed a deathly hush as we all - Ian excepted - took in what had just happened, and tried to think of something helpful to say to ease the insult. The moment was broken by Eric, who had the presence of mind to press the button to start the camera and call "Rolling!"

Eric enjoyed set-ups where I was in an uncomfortable position. "It keeps the interviews short," he would say with a grin. On this occasion I remember getting cramp part way through, but aside from my discomfort everything went well. Until, that is, I spotted the river of liquid mud flowing from Jim's boots onto the carpet. Well, river might be a slight exaggeration, but there was no denying the small pond that was being created. Jim attempted an apology. "We seem to be making a bit of a mess of your carpet," he said. I felt annoyed at being included in what was Jim's own creation, and gave him a withering look as I said, "I think you're being unnecessarily plural." The Chief Minister smiled broadly, and assured us it wasn't a problem. I shook hands and thanked him for his time, and we picked up the equipment and began heading back towards the lift. As we left his office and started down the corridor, resplendent in its beautiful and very expensive carpet, I was immediately filled with a sense of horror. Imprinted into the luxurious, deep blue pile was the outline of a pair of boots coming the other way, each step having left behind a perfect stamp of the footprint in mud. Jim had, quite literally, left his mark on the building. I had, for many years, spent a lot of time and effort getting to know the most important people on the island and building a reputation with them, both for myself and my company. I could see the results of that work dissolving before my eyes as I followed the imprints back to the lift. A few harsh words were said as we descended, but by the time we made it back to the hotel the incident had been put behind us.

I usually stayed at the Palace Hotel on the prom in Douglas, which meant that I knew its layout very well. The Rotary lunch for Hugh Williams was being held in the main function room, and to get there guests had to pass through the Round Bar. Its entrance was a choke point. You entered through double doors in a corner of the room, but immediately had to turn left because there was a wall about ten feet in front of you. The organisers of the lunch had compounded matters by putting their registration desk in this entrance area, making the choke point even tighter. It was a situation I was about to use to my advantage. Our camera had a large sticker on the side with the title *Border Television* boldly displayed. I told Jim to mount it on the tripod and place it in the entrance so that everyone coming through the door would immediately see the company name and logo. This, I thought, was chutzpah at its best, and would show in a humorous, cheeky way that the BBC had strong competition from us. We retired to my favourite table and sat back to watch what would unfold. Within a few minutes the Rotary's reception staff turned up, and there was much pointing at the camera. Shortly afterwards, David, the hotel's manager came across. Taking care to keep his back to the organisers so they couldn't see his grinning expression, he told me that they had complained. I smiled at him and said, "And what did you say?" He said that he'd explained we worked very hard, and surely were allowed some time to have lunch. "And where else could you put the camera?" he asked. "Thanks," I replied. "I think I owe you a drink." "Not at all," he said. "I'll get you one. I haven't had so much fun in years!" And so arrived the first of many tipples we enjoyed that lunchtime. It seemed everyone who came through the door stopped to look at the camera. There was much gesturing and laughing. A few who knew me cast glances around the Round Bar to search me out. They knew that only I would pull a stunt like this. And half a dozen or so bought me a congratulatory drink. It turned into a very jolly lunch. I never did meet Hugh Williams, so I don't know if he found it quite as funny as everyone else.

We had a minor celebration when the interview with Douglas Hurd appeared on ITN's News at One. I'd overcome some pretty difficult obstacles to get it but, like much of television, the work involved in creating it is rarely appreciated on-screen. That afternoon at five o'clock we turned up at Government Buildings for the pre-arranged press conference, and I was introduced to the Home Secretary. He scrutinised me for a moment before a smile broke out on his face. "You were the chap at the airport this morning," he said. "I was." The Home Secretary's smile broadened. "Well done," he said with a laugh. "I thought it was hilarious!"

The other memorable charter flight to the Isle of Man came about with similar haste. On this occasion I was preparing to travel south to see an old friend ahead of that year's TT races. Dave Saville was a sidecar rider who'd already won a number of TT titles. He'd agreed for us to mount a camera on his unit during racing, and we were headed off to work out the engineering that would be needed to make it all work. Back then, it was a novel exercise that no-one had undertaken before. The equipment was bulky and fragile, and there were several levels of testing we had to carry out before we could be reasonably sure of success. In the end our camera never lost a race, and completed the first 100 miles an hour lap for a sidecar. It was an enviable record. But sadly our friend Dave crashed at Creg ny Baa during a Manx Grand Prix classic race, and died some years later from his injuries.

Before we could get on our way, I got a request from the newsroom. A fishing boat from Whitehaven had sunk off the Isle of Man during the night, and the survivors were being treated in Noble's Hospital in Douglas. Our local team couldn't get an interview with them, so I was asked if I would go across and sort things out. As is often the case, the logistics came first. It involved hiring two aircraft and two cars, and called on the services of the company driver, Robin. One aircraft would take us from Carlisle to the Isle of Man, where I'd pick up a car from our usual hire company. We'd then be able to get around the island to film. Another aircraft would then take us to Blackpool to meet up with Robin, who would have brought our film vehicle down from Carlisle. He'd then use a hire car to get home. There might have been better ways to organise it, but this allowed me to do what I needed to do as efficiently as possible, while being as helpful as I could to my colleagues in news.

During the period when I was going to the Isle of Man most regularly, someone came up with a bright idea to save money. The crew vehicles we used to transport us and our equipment around had just been changed for newer models, and one of the cameramen suggested it would save us having to hire vehicles on the island if we based the recently retired one there instead. It turned out to be a less than stellar move, for two unforeseen reasons. The first was fairly straightforward, while the second caused me much laughter when I eventually worked out what was going on.

The old blue Volkswagen Caravelle was taken across on the ferry, and an arrangement was made to store it and make sure it would start whenever we came to use it. I have to say that I hated this particular vehicle, and was extremely disappointed that it wasn't being scrapped. It had a noisy air-cooled engine in the back, right behind my seat, and the worst heating system I'd ever encountered, so my feet were permanently cold in winter. Its arrival on the island came just a few months ahead of my move from the role of a reporter and presenter to that of a producer/director, and since I was the driving force behind covering Manx news, the number of trips, and therefore the usefulness of having a vehicle based there, fell dramatically. This enthusiasm for the Isle of Man was much appreciated, and Eddie Lowey, a member of the Legislative Council, once confided in me that he was contemplating putting forward the idea of an honours system for the island. He said he wanted me to be the first recipient. I wasn't sure whether he was teasing me, but I was a bit embarrassed by the suggestion. Ultimately I was spared the decision of whether or not I would accept, since nothing came of his plans.

During the time the blue Caravelle lived on the Isle of Man I began to notice something rather odd. As we drove around in it, the drivers of other cars would wave. I remember once sitting in a crew van at a set of traffic lights just off Tottenham Court Road in London when someone tapped on my window and said thanks for working so hard for them. It turned out that they held shares in the company, and were delighted that the price was steadily rising. But that vehicle was liveried with the company name, and easily recognisable. The blue Caravelle wasn't. Often, if you buy a new car, you'll become aware suddenly of how many of that model and colour there are on the road. Similarly, once I noticed the first one or two waves, they seemed to come thick and fast, and I began to puzzle over why we'd become so popular.

The clue which finally led me to the answer came when we arrived for one particular filming trip. We loaded everything into the vehicle and the driver turned the key to start the engine. The Volkwagen's air-cooled unit was never particularly quiet or smooth, but the racket which issued forth this time could only have been caused by something terminal. It was clear that we were sitting in an ex-crew vehicle. My first thought was how to solve the problem of getting around, so I arranged to hire a replacement and we went on our way. But my mind was working the clues. How could an engine fail when the van had been sitting doing nothing for weeks on end? After a while I thought I had it worked out, though I was never able to prove the theory, and I felt it better to let the matter drop. I'd noticed that a high proportion of the vehicles we were attracting waves from were taxis. Could it be possible that the Caravelle was being used as a taxi during the times we weren't there to use it ourselves? The other taxi drivers were acknowledging our vehicle rather than its occupants. It would also explain why we'd encountered a broken, well-used engine when it had been relatively healthy the last time we'd been there. I never did discover whether my detective skills were accurate. Sometimes it's best not to know.

We arrived on the chartered flight at Ronaldsway Airport, picked up the hire car, and made for the island's main hospital in Douglas. We ran into the local cameraman and reporter when we got there, both wearing rather glum faces. In many ways I felt for them. They had to live and operate within the Manx system, and were forced to endure pressures that I, as an outsider, was immune from. It wasn't simply that they were less experienced. Rather, they were hampered by being seen as locals. I could play the part of what the Manx call the off-comer, which had distinct advantages. The main one was that I was much harder to say no to. I searched out the hospital administrator, explained who I was, and that I'd like access to the group who'd been rescued. I was surprised by his slightly aggressive response. He refused point-blank, and told me to leave his hospital. Dealing with people in this situation calls for an instinctive approach. Do you respond with equal or greater aggression, or do you take a softer, more conciliatory approach? On this occasion I went for the latter. I agreed with him that the people who'd been plucked from the Irish Sea in the early hours of the morning probably wouldn't want to be bothered by us, but would he at least be prepared to go and ask them? I guess he saw this as an ideal way to get rid of us, so he agreed. But the response he got from them was not what he expected.

Border Television was very close to the communities it served, and although I had moved on from my time in front of the camera, my face was still well remembered. Ours was a small station - the second smallest in the ITV network - and for the most part our viewers regarded us as friends. So when the administrator asked if they wanted to be interviewed for the local news programme, the boat's crew were happy to agree. I could see a look of puzzlement on his face when he came back to tell me, and I was very careful to be gracious in victory.

It turned out that the group were raising money for charity, and the fishing boat had been the support vessel for a couple of guys rowing across the Irish Sea in a bathtub. When their rescuers had found them, they were astonished by the sight of a group of men clinging to the upturned bath. As I spoke with them, I realised how shocked they actually were. What had begun as a jolly jape had come close to claiming their lives, and the reality of their close escape had hit home by the time we arrived. One of them explained that he thought they might have lasted another hour, but no more. I felt a genuine compassion for their plight, and made them an offer which overjoyed them. I explained how our day had been interrupted by their story, and that we were really headed for the Midlands. Since we had an aircraft waiting to take us to Blackpool Airport, would they like a lift? I could arrange for Robin to drop them off in Whitehaven on his way home. It was as if I had lifted the blanket of cloud to let the sunshine in. They were delighted, and by the end of a day which had begun with them being unceremoniously dunked in the Irish Sea, they slept the sleep of the righteous back home in the safety of their own beds. I never heard from them again, but I was pleased to help them out. It brought to mind a line penned by one of my favourite song writers, Paul Williams. *Every act of kindness is a little bit of love we leave behind.* That night I felt I'd extended a little kindness to some people who desperately needed it. And it felt good.

As I travelled around the region there would be

days when the sound recordist spent most of his time, it seemed, shaking his head with irritation during interviews as the peace and tranquility of the countryside was shattered by the arrival of another RAF fast jet cutting a path through the hills. The Lake District and Scottish borders were popular places for honing low flying skills, and the presence of an electronic warfare range in Northumberland ensured a steady flow of aircraft skimming above our heads at 200 feet as they made their way there. The low flying tactic was introduced to overcome the threat from enemy surface-to-air missile systems in a war, with aircraft hiding in the ground clutter amongst the hills and valleys. It led to some spectacular sights. One day we were parked at the peak of one of the passes in the south of the Lake District enjoying a break for lunch. Suddenly, there was an almighty roar and the windscreen was filled with an RAF jet travelling at high speed. I felt like I could have reached out and touched it. But what made this incident stand out from the many others I saw was that the aircraft was upside down.

I mentioned what I'd seen to an RAF pilot I met some time later and he wasn't surprised. He told me about an annual air combat exercise at Nellis Air Force Base in Nevada, not far from the glittering lights of Las Vegas. Britain's pilots are amongst those who take part in a three week campaign there which simulates a wartime environment. There's a huge amount of competition between those from the various nations taking part to be the best. He explained that one of the issues faced when flying low is the way that you deal with the ridges you have to cross between valleys. When the pilot pulls up the nose of the aircraft to climb over one he loses sight of the ground, and can inadvertently end up higher than he wants to be, with the potential for exposing the aircraft to a radar system. The answer the RAF came up with was to invert during the climb over the ridge so that the pilot could still see the ground below, and so judge his flight path more accurately. He smiled as he told me that it proved to be a very successful tactic which, in his words, "blew the Americans' minds". It certainly had that effect on me when I witnessed it atop that Lake District pass.

Perhaps the most spectacular sight of a low flying jet came as we were travelling back home along the M6 one afternoon at the end of a day's filming. We must all have been weary, because the constant drum of tyres on tarmac had sent all but the driver to sleep. We'd reached the Howgills, a small range of hills south of Tebay, when I awoke. I love the Howgills. These softly contoured mounds were always a sign, when I'd been away filming for days or weeks, that I was nearly home. Their curved shapes were like sleeping giants waiting to welcome me, and when the sun gets low in the western sky it creates an effect of light and shade on the undulating landscape which can only be described as breathtaking. The motorway winds its way through these hills for perhaps five miles, sharing the confines of the narrow Lune Valley with the west coast rail line and the river, two hundred feet below. As I opened my eyes I took in the scene around me. Outside was the familiar sight of the sculptured panorama. Inside, the electrician was asleep beside me, while the sound recordist snoozed in the front passenger seat. I watched in silence, savouring the relative peace after a day of hard work, as the driver negotiated the long bends. He glanced to his right, checking the door mirror for overtaking traffic. And then he did a double take. Curious, I turned around and looked behind me out of the back window to see what had attracted his attention, and the next few seconds will stay with me for the rest of my life. Picking its way through the hills to my right, flying at the same height we were driving, was the pterodactyl shape of a Vulcan. This last survivor of the three V-bombers built to carry Britain's nuclear weapons seemed to fill the valley. It was maneuvering hard as it turned to follow the gap through the gorge, and the world seemed to switch to slow motion as it slid by. I felt I had a special relationship with this mighty aeroplane. I'd first seen one at an airshow on Teesside a decade or more before. In a well practised routine it had snuck up behind the crowd as they watched the end of an aerobatic display. When the announcer introduced it, the aircraft was already over the airfield fence. The pilot called for full thrust from the four Olympus jet engines and pulled the massive bomber into a hard climb. Nobody who has heard the Vulcan carry out this manoeuvre can fail to have been impressed by the sound. It's an experience rather than simply a noise, vibrating your entire body as the power of the engines pushes the massive airframe skywards. From the back seat of the company Volvo I watched in awe as the delta-winged monster swept onwards and out of the valley, its pilot blissfully unaware of the effect he'd had on those who'd seem him fly by.

Sadly, the Vulcan was taken out of service in 1984 and airfields around the country began to take delivery of them to act as gate guardians. I stood on the roof of the control tower at Carlisle Airport as XJ823 made her last delivery flight there. The pilot was Squadron Leader Neil McDougall, and he told me of his long association with the aircraft. It had been one of the first Vulcans he'd flown, and had served as a conventional bomber and a nuclear bomber before being adapted to carry Blue Steel, Britain's nuclear stand-off missile. My news report on the day can still be found on YouTube, and I recall that, shortly before I interviewed Neil, one of my friends at the airport whispered in my ear that he'd been involved in the Falklands War. Neil was flying a mission in XM597 to fire Shrike missiles at Port Stanley Airfield when the refueling probe broke. With not enough fuel remaining to return to Ascension Island, he opted to divert to Rio de Janeiro. Despite firing off one of the missiles to reduce drag - the other one stuck on the pylon - and climbing higher to increase fuel efficiency, he landed with just enough fuel for one more circuit of the airfield. Neil was very laid back about the incident, though I suspect it got his attention at the time. The diversion made headlines around the world.

Twenty-one years after XJ823 arrived at Carlisle, I watched the last remaining flying Vulcan, XH558, at the Blackpool airshow. This was to be its final year performing for the crowds, and in a poignant scene back at Carlisle Airport three months later, she flew over XJ823 in a last salute to the V-bombers. There was a lump in my throat as I watched the smoke trail from her engines disappear towards the Lake District, knowing I'd never see one of these magnificent aircraft in the sky again.

The low flying activities of the RAF were controversial at times. There were regular training accidents, and since I had some aviation knowledge I was often sent to report on the aftermath. This led to an another experience which I'll never forget. I arranged to go and film at a training squadron to understand why low flying was necessary. It was a long journey which took me to RAF Lossiemouth in the north of Scotland. On the banks of the Moray Firth, the air base was home to the Operational Conversion Unit which trained pilots on the Jaguar ground attack aircraft. It was also home to a search and rescue squadron, and the aircraft which provided an airborne early warning system. The plan was that we would film activities with the Jaguar squadron, and my cameraman would be taken for a flight in the back seat of one of the dual-seat trainers. After our long drive north we were introduced to the team, and it was at this point my cameraman decided to drop a bombshell. He announced that he had a back problem and didn't want to fly. The workings of the ejection seat were being explained at the time, along with a warning that it could cause some temporary damage to the back if, as our briefer put it, they had to bang out. I'm not sure if the technician had a genuine problem with his back, or whether he simply got frightened at the prospect of what lay ahead. Either way, it didn't matter. I never asked anyone to do something I wasn't prepared to do myself, and this was an opportunity to prove it once more. So I immediately said I would go instead, and for the rest of the evening there was a broad grin on my face.

In my office at home there are two photographs taken the following day. Save for the length of my hair, you could be fooled into thinking I had served in the RAF. The first shows me standing in front of XX835, resplendent in my flying overalls and G-suit, and wearing a confident smile. Fast forward to the second image, taken a few minutes later. By now I'm sitting in the back seat of the aircraft, having donned a flying helmet and oxygen mask. There's very little of my face visible, so it's likely few people would spot the difference in expression. Only my eyes reveal the change. Gone is the confidence, and in its place is a look of some concern. But the change in demeanour didn't come about from any realisation of what I was about to experience. Rather it was because of what I had already faced. The cockpit was a long way off the ground, and the only way to get there was to climb up a ladder. I should remind you at this point that I'm afraid of heights.

Soon we were lined up on the runway, and the pilot

was giving me a running commentary on what he was doing. I think I have something of a brain disorder which means my memory is skewed towards the retention of number information. I can forget someone's name within ten seconds of being introduced to them. Once when I mentioned the affliction to a professor in Liverpool he smiled and told me I had Nominal Aphasia. Perhaps he smiled because I had just forgotten his name. But despite this deficiency I have no trouble in remembering the name of the pilot I flew with that day, not just because this was a unique experience in my life, but also because his name was one you simply couldn't forget. He was Squadron Leader Jock Stirrup, destined to become Air Chief Marshal and Chief of the Defence Staff. Now retired, he sits in the House of Lords as Baron Stirrup.

What I didn't know about Jock would have allayed any niggling fears I might have had about the flight ahead. He had previously been on loan to the Sultan of Oman's Air Force and had gained combat experience in the Dhofar War. Six months before I met him he'd been checking out the progress of a student from the back seat of his Jaguar when they suffered a bird strike which shattered the canopy and started an engine fire. While many would have ejected at this point, he chose to stay with the aircraft, not knowing whether the front seat student was still conscious. Showing great skill and courage, Jock managed to land the aircraft safely at RAF Leuchars in Fife. In recognition of his actions he was awarded the Air Force Cross. I couldn't have been in safer hands.

Visibility from the back seat of the Jaguar was excellent. I was much higher than the front seat occupant and had an unobstructed view over his head. I also had a full set of flying controls, and as he prepared to take off Jock warned me to keep my feet flat on the floor and away from the rudder pedals. With the brakes applied, he wound the engines up to full power. The Turbomeca Adour turbofans pushed hard, before Jock selected the afterburners and released the brakes. We were off, accelerating hard down the runway. This was a world away from my own flying experience. I was used to a somewhat leisurely take-off as a 180 horse-power piston engine turned a propeller in front of me to drag us through the air. Acceleration was not what you would call brisk, and I would begin to rotate at around 60 miles an hour. In the Jaguar it was all happening faster than I could take in, and before I knew it we had blown a long way past 100 miles an hour and were airborne. But then an odd thing happened. We didn't immediately begin climbing steeply. Instead, there was a short, gentle altitude gain before we levelled off, and when I glanced down at the instruments I could see that we were travelling at 420 knots just 250 feet above the ground.

I found very quickly that I could only manage to look forwards, in the direction of travel. Any attempt to look out to the side of the aircraft gave my brain too much information to process, such was the sensation of speed.

But it didn't seem to bother Jock. He continued to give me a running commentary on what was happening, interspersed with the occasional question and a glance in the mirror to check I was surviving the experience. I eventually remembered the reason I was there and began to shoot some film. Television technology was a bit antiquated at the time, and the film camera I was carrying in my lap was a very basic affair with less than three minutes of usable film in it. The cameraman had guessed at an exposure setting before I left, so all I had to do was point and shoot. But before long I began to feel uncomfortable. My temperature was rising and I was very aware that I must have been given the visitors' oxygen mask. Over the unpleasant smell of rubber was an unmistakable odour of vomit, kindly donated by the last passenger who'd been taken for a flight. I'd had the sense to eat very little for breakfast, and had been warned that, whatever my flying experience, I would certainly be sick. So I unclipped the mask and obeyed the instructions of my body. I felt much better after that, and took more of an interest in the world around me again. I marvelled at the abilities of Jock in the front seat. Flying this aircraft fast and low was hard enough, but the additional pressure of going to war in it and accomplishing the assigned mission was way beyond my comprehension.

We completed a low level circuit of north and west Scotland, and soon I could see the Moray Firth reappear on the horizon. As we crossed the shoreline and began to head out across the water, Jock eased back on the stick and the aircraft effortlessly climbed to 3,000 feet. He then said something to me which I will never forget. "Would you like to fly her?" For a moment I was shocked by the idea, but then I heard myself reply, "Yes please." In what I had done hundreds of times in my pilot training, I went through the procedure for taking over the aircraft. "You have control," said Jock. "I have control," I said. And now I was flying an RAF fast jet. I couldn't believe it. The Jaguar felt beautiful as it cut through the air, the controls light and responsive as I carefully manoeuvered it around. The sky was bright blue, and I could look down at the ripples on the surface of the water far below, and see the coastline of the Moray Firth off to my left. And then an even more extraordinary thing happened. Something caught my eye ahead, and it quickly resolved into another aircraft coming towards us. "Contact ahead, one o'clock level," I reported to Jock. "Seen it," came the response. At a closing speed of around a thousand miles an hour I watched an RAF Buccaneer pass by on the right-hand side, just a few hundred feet away. It seemed that my brain was operating in two modes. One part was calm and in control, feeling the aircraft as it responded to my gentle inputs to keep it under control. The other was shouting with pleasure, unable to comprehend what I was doing.

All too soon it came to an end. "Fuel's getting low," said Jock. "Time to go home. I have control." "You have control," I responded with a hint of sadness in my voice, and we began the descent, turning to head back to Lossiemouth. It's not easy to express the exhilaration I felt that day, and the privilege I had been afforded. How many civilians had been in a Jaguar? And how many had actually flown this graceful, powerful war machine? My thoughts were drawn to the words of an American pilot serving with the Canadian Air Force in the Second World War. Captain John Gillespie Magee, Jr. was only 19 years old at the time of his death, but he is remembered for his beautiful poem, *High Flight*. In it, Magee captures the joy of flying, expressing the emotions and sensations, the freedom and grace of movement, in a manner that leaves me envious of his use of language.

Oh, I have slipped the surly bonds of earth
And danced the skies on laughter-silvered wings;
Sunward I've climbed, and joined the tumbling mirth
Of sun-split clouds - and done a hundred things
You have not dreamed of - wheeled and soared and swung
High in the sunlit silence. Hov'ring there,
I've chased the shouting wind along, and flung
My eager craft through footless halls of air.
Up, up the long, delirious, burning blue
I've topped the windswept heights with easy grace
Where never lark, or even eagle flew.
And while with silent, lifting mind I've trod
The high untrespassed sanctity of space,
Put out my hand, and touched the face of God.

Tragically, Captain John Magee was killed within a few months of sending the poem to his parents back home in the United States when his Spitfire collided with another aircraft in the cloudy skies above war-torn England. His legacy is a work of art which should be a mandatory read for every trainee pilot, an inspirational taste of the joys that lie in wait.

We landed, and Jock deployed the parachute at the rear of the aircraft to slow us. He turned off the runway, and with a dexterous touch released the 'chute, before blowing it away with a quick blast of the engines so the ground crew could retrieve it with ease. We arrived back at the stand, and a ladder was attached to the side of the cockpit, the canopy by now pointing to the part of the sky where I'd been in ecstasy just a few short minutes before. As happened so many times in my career, an experience had altered me. That change may have been very subtle, but in some small way my flight with Jock had made me a different person. A member of the ground crew appeared at the top of the ladder beside me and disconnected the various hoses and cables which attached me to the aircraft. He reached for my oxygen mask and I resisted. Feeling slightly embarrassed, I explained what was in it. "Don't worry about it," he said. "Every passenger throws up." He helped me out of the aircraft, having first replaced the pins which prevented the ejection seat from firing, and I discovered the fear of heights which previously had made entry into the Jaguar a challenge had, at least temporarily, disappeared.

When my feet reached the ground I felt a weakness in

my legs. The flight had taken a huge toll on my energy levels, and when the adrenaline began to dissipate I was left doing a passable impression of a jelly. I walked unsteadily back to the squadron office and changed out of my flying suit. The crew were helpful and attentive, displaying an understanding of the way my body had reacted. I was taken for coffee and some lunch, spending the time alone in my own world, lost in the realisation of what I had just done, unwilling and unable to let it slip from reality to memory. Jock and his team were kindness personified, keeping a watchful eye on me as my recovery process began. By the time the meal was over I had begun to engage more with those around me, and eventually glanced at my watch before announcing that we'd better get on with work. There was still much to film. I could see a look of disappointment on the faces of the crew. It was the electrician who explained their reaction. "They told us that you would come back from the flight so wiped out that you'd be out of it for the rest of the day," he said. "We've been looking forward to a quiet afternoon." "Fat chance," I thought. But I felt an unaccountable sense of pride that I'd shown a faster than average response time. Maybe I had the makings of a proper pilot after all.

I have a few treasured, tangible memories of that day. The two photographs of me with the aircraft are displayed in a suitably prominent position. Jock presented me with a Jaguar shoulder patch as evidence that I had joined an elite club. And to cement the experience formally in the annals of aviation, he entered it in my pilot's log book, an official document recording my every flight. In black ink from an italic-nibbed fountain pen, the entry for 21st October 1983 shows a flight from 10:10 to 11:05 GMT in a Jaguar T Mk 2, XX835, from RAF Lossiemouth. The captain's name is recorded as Squadron Leader Stirrup. But what makes the entry so special are the contents of three of the line's columns. One, in the section for daytime flights in a multi-engined aircraft, shows a duration of fifty-five minutes in the column marked Dual or P2. In the column for the Holder's Operating Capacity Jock entered *P. U/T*, shorthand for Pilot Under Training. And on the far right is his signature with the annotation *Certified Correct*. His kindness in recording the flight in this way provides me with enduring evidence that I have officially undertaken fifty-five minutes of training in an RAF fast jet.

There are two postscripts to that historic flight. The first came the following week when I was preparing to edit the film. For reasons I can only speculate on, the cameraman reported events at Lossiemouth to his union. You'll recall that he didn't want to fly because he claimed to have a bad back, and was fearful of how it would be affected in the unlikely event of an ejection. The local technicians' union was particularly militant, and from my perspective at least, seemed intent on doing as much as possible to disrupt the normal operations of the company. It was, therefore, not surprising that they enthusiastically voted to outlaw the use of the film I had shot, and it was discarded without being processed.

I don't remember being particularly upset at the time. The members of the union's controlling clique were like characters from that wonderful Peter Sellers film *I'm Alright Jack*, and just as ridiculously hilarious. There's a tale to be told about their antics, but it's best saved for another tome to ensure the real Fred Kite and his comrades are honoured sufficiently for their disservice to the television industry. Interestingly, when the power of the unions waned, their place was inherited by the health and safety brigade. There seems to be a part of the personality of some people who crave power which tempts them into the misuse of it for their own ends. It's not an approach which particularly appeals or endears them to me.

The second codicil took place later, at the end of August the following year. I had completed a further phase of flying training, and this required my log book to go to the Civil Aviation Authority for the issuance of the new rating I had earned. In due course it was returned and I leafed through, examining the various stamps which had been placed in it and signed by flying instructors across the years. To my fury I discovered a pencil notation below Squadron Leader Stirrup's validation of my fifty-five minutes of flying time with him. Some civil servant had written *Hardly!* on the page. I didn't quite know what to do, and mentioned it to a friend at the airport who was a more experienced flyer than me. "How would he know?" he asked. "Was he there?" So it was with some relish that I set about erasing this stain on my character and my logbook with the use of a rubber on the end of a pristine new yellow pencil. I felt vindicated at the time, but all these years later I wonder if I should have left it there as evidence of just how exceptional - and for some, unbelievable - my time at RAF Lossiemouth had been. After all, who could challenge my claim when I could call on the Chief of the Defence Staff to verify it?

Six years later I had a further encounter with the Jaguar. By now I was a producer and director, and had decided to revisit the subject of low flying within the context of a half hour programme. This time I was invited south to RAF Coltishall in Norfolk, which was home to four squadrons of Jaguars. Our visit was hosted by the friendly guys at 54 Squadron, led by Squadron Leader DIM Jones. They were all instantly likeable, and we enjoyed our time with them. I was always particularly keen to demonstrate an openness and honesty when working with the armed services. I never had anything to do with the Navy, but filmed on a number of occasions with the Army and the Royal Air Force. The RAF guys always seemed more laid back, but I never fully understood what brought about the difference in culture. One thing was certain. Whichever service they were a part of, the personnel I met always had an outsized sense of humour.

On one occasion a few years earlier I had taken a news crew to report on a military exercise in south-west Scotland. I can't say it was huge fun for us, and I'm sure the soldiers taking part shared that view. It must have been sometime in Spring, because the first vestiges of light were expected around 6 am, and we set off cold and sleepy very early to get there in time. The first part of the exercise was due to be held on a disused airfield which would be used to land paratroopers. A number of Hercules transport aircraft were due to arrive as dawn broke, and a bunch of brave guys would leap out of them to start the make-believe war. We were with a large force of troops on the ground, though I'm not sure exactly why they were there. However, as the appointed hour approached we were all in place, shivering slightly, and in my case at least, longing for the warm and comfortable bed I'd left what seemed like a long time previously. It was a difficult task for the cameraman. Whilst there was some light beginning to fill the sky, the ground was dark. We still worked on film at this time, and he needed some idea of what aperture to set on the camera's lens. Unlike with video cameras, the viewfinder only showed you what was in the frame, not how bright it was. So he asked the electrician to turn on the hand basher. This quaintly named piece of equipment is a hand-held light, powered by a large and heavy battery. Paul flicked the switch, and suddenly the open field ahead of us was bathed in light. Immediately, the squaddies let out a concerted, delighted cheer. We were not the only people checking our equipment ahead of the action. Their Commanding Officer was caught in the middle of the field relieving himself. I'm sure that military training at Sandhurst must have omitted the advice to avoid having a wee in a field when there's a film crew around. I made sure to stay away from him for the rest of the day, but the incident certainly made us a lot of friends amongst the soldiers around us.

DIM Jones explained that a group of the guys from 54 Squadron were going into Norwich that night for a Valentine's Day curry, which seemed to be an annual event. Would we like to go? It was a kind offer. It gave us an opportunity to get to know each other, and I readily agreed. There were more than a dozen in the group, and when we arrived at the chosen restaurant we were shown to a room at the back. Presently, a waiter came and took our order for food before returning with drinks. I chatted with people around the table, and it turned into a perfect, convivial evening. Well, nearly perfect. Because, ninety minutes later we were still waiting for our food. Eventually one of the pilots became so frustrated that he left and walked across the road to a take-away, bringing back a curry which he graciously shared with the rest of us. I was grateful for the food, but annoyed I hadn't thought of the idea myself. But eventually, the food we'd ordered turned up and my appetite was fully satisfied.

The following day we began filming. On this occasion, it was decided that none of my team would fly. But the squadron had a camera which they would fly for us, operated by one of the pilots from the back seat. It turned out really well, and I was delighted with the results. DIM even arranged to carry out a practice attack on the control tower at Carlisle Airport so that our viewers would have something to recognise in the finished programme. While we were in the operations room where flights were planned, my cameraman, Eric, mentioned that he got annoyed when fast jets flew low over his house. He lived in the countryside, and he said that it seemed he was on some sort of flight path for low flying military aircraft. DIM expressed sympathy, and asked Eric to show him where his house was on the detailed map of Cumbria attached to the ops room wall. Eric saw this as an opportunity to reduce the annoyance factor and return some peace to his rural location. He pointed to his bungalow on the map, and DIM drew a red circle around it with a wax pencil. "That'll get you sorted," he said. We had an enjoyable stay with 54 Squadron, and a couple of days later headed back on the long drive home.

As with the visit to RAF Lossiemouth, there were two postscripts to the visit. The following week Eric was off work. He was a keen gardener and had taken a few days holiday to tidy up his plot in preparation for the start of the growing season. He was grateful for some good weather, and toiled away tirelessly. But by the end of Monday he was aware that something unusual was afoot. With monotonous regularity a seemingly endless stream of military jets flashed by just above his head, and although he thought he was being paranoid at first, it became obvious they were targeting his house. As the days passed by, the procession of aircraft showed no sign of diminishing, and he was sure that if we had been in a war his cabbage patch would have been coleslaw by now. Eric had no real interest in aircraft, but even to his untrained eye these visitors all looked suspiciously like the Jaguars we'd been filming the previous week. On the Wednesday he called me in confusion, unable to work out what had changed to make his isolated house suddenly so popular, and I began to laugh. DIM Jones' red circle around the property wasn't an exclusion zone as Eric believed, but a target designation. And he must have passed the coordinates on to the commanders of the other Jaguar squadrons at RAF Coltishall so they could join in the game too. For the entire week, Eric's tranquil peace was shattered on an hourly basis as the next wave of attack aircraft zeroed in on him. Eventually DIM took pity and erased the red circle from around the house, but Eric made sure he would never again tell anyone where he lived.

The second postscript was some years later. I was making a programme about military technology as part of my international award-winning series *Innovators*, and I ended up at RAF Porton Down. I had gone to see a Harrier jump jet which was being used to test TIALD, Thermal Imaging and Laser Designation, a system designed to guide the new generation of smart bombs. I always like to find out about the people I meet, and chatted with the pilot about his experiences in the Air Force. He told me that he had switched to the Harrier only a few years before, having previously flown the Jaguar. I told him how friendly we'd found the guys at 54 Squadron, and launched into the story of the Valentine's Day curry bash. He listened patiently as I related the events of the evening, and of how we waited ages for the food to arrive. "It took so long to come," I explained, "that one pilot..." At that point he interrupted me and finished the sentence. "He went across the road and brought back a curry to share while you were waiting." I looked at him with astonishment. "How did you know that?" I asked. "Because that pilot was me," came the reply. We laughed about his stunt, and I marvelled, not for the first time, at how regularly my life was marked by these remarkable episodes of synchronicity.

One of the gentler forms of aviating I came into contact with was ballooning. There's something appealing about seeing a hot air balloon floating effortlessly across a summer sky, the silence of the moment only momentarily broken by the roar of the gas burner heating the air in the envelope. I had taken over responsibility for much of our non-news output, responding to a challenge to create a half-hour programme for most Friday nights in the year. It was a big ask, and called for a level of efficiency which hadn't been seen before, in the management of both time and budgets. I quickly learned that I could make some programmes for practically nothing, applying the savings I accrued to others which could be a little more spectacular. In the space of a year or so I made more than forty half-hours, and to the chagrin of those who were opposed to the idea, attained a greater than ten percent hit rate with industry awards. But there was almost an embarrassment on the part of some at my achievements. It was almost as if they didn't want these programmes to be a success.

In this spirit of efficiency I found what I thought would be a nice event to film in the south Lakes one Sunday. I was travelling that day to the Isle of Man to begin production of a programme on the Monday, and the flight was during Sunday evening. It made sense to do something useful to fill the rest of the day. That something was a hot air balloon festival, and I could see the images in my mind of the colourful and inventive shapes filling the sky. It turned out to be a fascinating day in the sunshine, and everyone I met and spoke with was very helpful. In time-honoured ballooning tradition we even chased after one pilot as the gentle breeze carried her in the direction it thought best. We worked hard in the hours available to us, yet at the end of filming as we left for our flight to the Isle of Man I felt I didn't have quite enough material for the programme I wanted to make. A week or two later I called one of the pilots I had met and asked if he was planning any more flights. He told me of one taking off from Shugborough Hall in Staffordshire, the former estate of the Earls of Lichfield. He would be launching two balloons on this particular morning, and I hatched a plan to put a presenter in one, and a camera in the other.

The best times for flying are often early in the morning and late in the evening, when the atmosphere is undisturbed. Some of my own most satisfying flights have been during the still of the evening, when the day's heat has subsided and the air is cool and calm. I was told to be at the estate at 5:30 am. The aim was to go flying at six. After a night in an unmemorable motel by a busy main road we turned up at the appointed hour, a little bleary eyed. The crews were already hard at work teasing the envelopes into life, using gas burners and large fans to inflate them. As they began to take shape an interesting conversation was had. My cameraman, Eric, shared my dislike of heights. Unlike me, he also hated flying. So he had two very good reasons not to get into the large wicker basket attached to the balloon, which looked like it was designed as an over-sized picnic hamper. He looked at me and said, "So what are we going to do?" This was code for, "Don't think for a minute that I'm going into the sky attached to that thing". I understood his anxiety, and wouldn't for a moment have tried to force him to do it. So I climbed into the basket and he passed the camera to me, before helping his sound recordist, Cliff, to follow. My presenter, Jane, got aboard the other balloon.

Soon we were airborne, and it was an experience unlike anything I'd ever encountered before. We hung there in the sky, drifting slowly eastwards, leaving the grandeur of Shugborough behind. I began to film, and Jane carried out an interview with the pilot of the other balloon about a quarter of a mile away using a radio microphone. I was so involved in what I was doing that I didn't feel any sense of fear, despite having nothing more than a few strips of willow between me and the long fall below. I was aware of a sense of peace I had never before encountered on a flight. On commercial jets there's a constant noise from the engines, and a bustle in the cabin. In my own flying the aircraft was much noisier, and I would wear a headset with gel covers around the ears to seal out the intrusion. There's an isolation from the elements which support the weight of the aircraft, and you're caught in a hybrid state, partly operating a machine and partly communing with nature. Perhaps the nearest I'd come to the latter was when I encountered a bird while on a final approach. I was four miles out in the descent and everything was stable, set up to gently kiss the welcoming tarmac where the piano keys marked the beginning of the runway. And then I noticed a group of fellow travellers. A small flock of birds, four at most, crossed the nose of the aircraft just ahead, the final one in train presenting a conflict with my flight path. They all looked so elegant and delicate, at home in the environment where I was no more than a temporary stranger - an intruder. Without adjusting the engine power, I lifted the nose to avoid contact, and as I did I saw its head turn to look at me. There seemed no fear, just a curiosity, questioning the existence of this interloper and its purpose. And then we were past. I released pressure on the yoke and adjusted the attitude of the aircraft to reacquire the glide slope, glancing back to see with relief that the flock remained intact. It was to be my only interaction with nature in my powered flying career. In contrast, this journey presented an opportunity to discover the delights of flight devoid of mechanical noise.

The initial flurry of filming over, I took more of an interest in my surroundings. It was a beautiful morning, with blue skies and a warmth to the day despite the early hour. The landscape below was unfamiliar, but back to the west I could still see the magnificence of Shugborough Hall with the urban clutter of Stafford just visible in the distance beyond. Although we were making some progress across the ground, the breeze was slight, and there was a chance to relax and study the view. Below, a herd of deer grazed, unaware of our presence above. The world was coming awake, and I was in the perfect place to observe it. For a moment my focus moved to within the confines of my transport, examining the weave of the basket and the thickness of the ropes attaching it to the balloon. The basket's walls extended only to about waist height, yet I felt secure and surprisingly unconcerned about my position in space. I thought that Eric could probably have coped with this, but was grateful that we had swapped places. This was an experience to savour.

Beside me was Eric's sound recordist, Cliff. We shared an enthusiasm for flying, and I could see he was devouring the atmosphere. It seemed like perfection, a glorious start to the day, affording me a privileged position floating above the humdrum of life below. Very slowly we approached Blithfield Reservoir, a relatively recent addition to the landscape. I noticed the pilot hadn't used the gas burner for a while, and we were descending gently towards the water. I thought I could guess what was coming. With an inevitability brought about by the cooling of the air which kept us aloft, the bottom of the basket touched the water. Cliff swore and leapt to retrieve the camera batteries from the floor before they got wet. The pilot shared a smile with me, but the humour of the moment was lost on Cliff. Before temerity became tragedy the burner burst into life once more, and we rose from the surface of the reservoir to regain our rightful place in the sky, leaving the waters below to a trio of swans which gracefully alighted where we had just been.

We continued on in silence, conversation secondary to the need to absorb and enjoy every moment, every exquisite sight the view could offer. Time stretched and the world passed by. Life was seemingly sublime. But we knew this couldn't last forever, and eventually the pilot announced we were getting low on gas. By now the buildings on the edge of Burton-on-Trent were below us. This is a place renowned for its historical importance in the brewing industry. For a time in the 19th century, a quarter of all British beer came from here. I was a little surprised it wasn't a place of pilgrimage for Eric. As we slowly drifted earthwards I could see it was rush hour in Burton. Time had passed faster than I'd realised. The streets into the town were blocked with stationary traffic as people headed for work and children were driven to school. I was puzzled that the balloon was headed directly for the congestion, until I remembered that the pilot had little control over the direction of travel. That was decided for us by the wind. We descended lower until I could see the faces of drivers peering up at us through their windscreens, attracted by the occasional gas burn to control the speed of descent. Astonishingly, for me and for the drivers below, we appeared to be heading for a landing on the grassed centre of a roundabout on one of the town's arterial roads. This promised to be interesting. Landing an aircraft is much easier than a balloon. With an aeroplane you can add and reduce power as necessary to choose a landing spot to a high degree of accuracy. But with a balloon you only have control through the addition of lift. The descent is dependent upon the cooling of air in the envelope, a variable that's out of the pilot's control. Perhaps it was a miscalculation. Perhaps the centre of the roundabout was just too small a target to hit. Whatever the reason, as the drivers stuck in traffic watched in disbelief, it became obvious we weren't going to make it. We were less than ten feet off the ground, in danger of landing atop a car on the far side of the roundabout, when the pilot decided to abort the approach. He turned on the burner and the addition of hot air took us skyward once more. But not for long. By now the gas level was becoming critical, so he began a second attempt to land. The aiming point was just as close to a transport feature, but this time it was a canal. I was hoping against hope that I wouldn't see a repeat of events at Blithfield Reservoir. Water, basket, camera and me wasn't destined to be a happy mix. We were back down to about fifty feet, which so happened to be the height of the roofs of the houses on the edge of the canal. We scraped across the top of one, dislodging a chimney pot in the process. I was filming the final moments of the flight, but was doing so with a detached view of life. Looking through the viewfinder made it seem like I was watching events unfold on television, which I suppose I was. Again, I felt no fear. Finally we contacted the towpath with a bit more of a thump than was ideal, but we were down safely. The flight may not have been as exhausting as the one in the back seat of the Jaguar, but it had been every bit as thrilling.

A week or two later I put the programme together, and it remains on a short list of my favourites. It succeeded in capturing the serenity of the sport, and contained some beautiful images of multi-coloured hot air balloons against a crystal clear blue sky. I had long understood the importance of learning from previous errors, and was anxious to avoid a situation where the union committee would ban the pictures if it was discovered they hadn't been shot by one of their members. So we did the simplest thing possible and said nothing. The programme was duly broadcast and it was never an issue.

There was one other occasion when a balloon became the centre of my attention. It happened while I was a news reporter, and it involved a man whose company had probably built many of those at the Holker Hall festival, Per Lindstrand. He and Richard Branson got together in a mad-cap scheme to become the first people to cross the Atlantic Ocean in a hot air balloon. On July 2nd, 1987 they launched from Sugarloaf,

Maine on their epic adventure. The envelope was of a size never seen before, as tall as a 21-storey building, and encompassing more than two and a quarter million cubic feet of air. Soaring to 27,000 feet, it was carried east by the jet stream at 130 miles an hour. The balloon came onto my personal radar on the morning of July 3rd when I was set a challenge. *Go find Branson.* I needed no second invitation.

By then I'd held a pilot's licence for five years, and as a part of my training had been required to study and pass an exam on meteorology. This meant I had at least a basic understanding of weather systems, and it was this that led to a furious argument with Branson's press team. When I set about my task of tracking him down, I discovered he was approaching the north coast of Ireland heading due east, and the high pressure system he was flying through meant that, as he descended, he could only be pushed to the north of that track. It was basic stuff. Yet Branson's team was adamant that he would drift south to land somewhere in the north Midlands. I tried to explain why they were wrong, but they decided they knew better. The phone call ended shortly after that.

To track down the balloon I needed some transport, so I rang someone I knew at the local airport who trained military pilots. An ex-RAF squadron leader, he also bought former military helicopters and adapted them for civilian use. He was enthusiastic about the plan of action and I was soon on my way with a crew to meet up with him. Before we took off I studied the aeronautical chart of the area and told him we should head for Northern Ireland. He suggested we transit to Prestwick Airport on the west coast of Scotland to re-fuel on the way. Soon we were airborne and began heading north-west. Not long after departure we heard Branson's two support helicopters on the radio leaving Carlisle Airport for the north Midlands. Looking back, it's an odd measure of my confidence level that I didn't have a moment's doubt that I was right in my assessment of the situation and they were wrong. Perhaps I would have a greater sense of my fallibility today. However, as it turned out, that confidence was not misplaced. With full fuel tanks once more, we lifted from Prestwick to make the short crossing over the water to Northern Ireland. As we climbed towards the coast I looked to the south-east and a smile played on my lips. Approaching Prestwick in perfect formation were the two red support helicopters I'd seen an hour or so previously heading in the opposite direction. Clearly someone at Branson HQ had seen the light. I would wait in vain for any apology or thanks.

We were halfway across the water when an extraordinary thing happened. Above the noise of the engine and rotor blades I could faintly hear my cellphone ringing. It was one of the early models which cause much hilarity if they're seen in today's world of the smart phone. About the size of a brick, and not much lighter, my Motorola mobile was my pride and joy, and travelled everywhere with me in its designated space, a large pocket in my company-issued anorak. How I heard it I'll never know, but I did, and as I pressed the little green button to accept the call, the day went downhill. With the speaker cranked up to full volume I could just about make out the voice at the other end. It was with a sense of disbelief that I heard it say, after several requests from me to repeat words I missed, that I was to abandon the task and come back. I was stunned. How could they have as little faith in me as Branson's press office had shown? I was tempted for a moment to unscrew the extra-long antenna I'd fitted to the phone, designed to improve its performance, which would immediately drop the call. It was a ploy I'd used on occasions before when I didn't agree with the views of the newsdesk. I never could understand how someone sitting in an office, often a hundred miles away, thought they knew how the story was developing better than the reporter on the ground. Or, in this case, in the air. Dropping the call had been a convenient way of bringing debate to an end very swiftly. But in this instance I did what I was told. With not very good grace I hung up and told the pilot to reverse course. There was a stunned silence in the helicopter as everyone tried to understand why the decision had been made. But we turned around, and were soon heading for home. I sat looking out at the water below, fuming at the stupidity of the office, and starting to prepare for the argument I'd initiate on my return. And then the next extraordinary event played out in a day that was to be full of them. I heard the phone ring again. I came close to ignoring it, but decided in the end to discover the next genius of an that idea was going to be thrust at me. I was definitely not in the best of moods by now. Once again, I heard The Voice faintly above the noise of the helicopter. This time I asked it to repeat what it said to me, not so much because it was very faint, but because I couldn't believe what I was being told. In a decision which could have been written for a scene straight out of Blackadder, the Generals had reconvened and changed their collective mind. I'm not sure whether I responded before pushing the red button to end the call, but there was a mixture of ironic laughter and some bad language from all in the aircraft as I told the pilot to turn around again. We'd probably been travelling in the wrong direction for ten minutes or so before the second call came. The twenty minutes of fuel we'd wasted on the fruitless volte-face would cost us dearly later.

We continued westwards and were soon over dry land. But how do you find an albeit huge balloon in a vast, open sky? The answer was delivered in a timely manner by a friend I knew from the airport. He had been the one who had offered advice when the Civil Aviation Authority's civil servant queried the entry in my log book which showed just under an hour of training in the Jaguar, signed by the squadron leader I'd flown with. James and I had both travelled to Prestwick to sit an exam for the most basic of Air Traffic Controller's licences a few years previously so that we could operate the control tower at Carlisle Airport at weekends. In the intervening period he had advanced his training and credentials, and by a supreme coincidence was working the sector we were flying in, controlling aircraft from his seat at the Scottish Air Traffic Control Centre. When our pilot first made contact, I immediately recognised his voice, and asked John to identify us and tell him what we were doing. Helpful as always, James provided us with the information we needed. My heart leapt when I hear his next transmission. "The balloon is in your twelve o'clock, range two miles," he announced. I had put the cameraman in the front left seat of the Gazelle helicopter so his camera had an unrestricted view. I was in the seat behind him, and leant forward so that I could scan the sky ahead and above. I could see nothing but a light grey overcast about fifteen hundred feet above. But as I watched, the view began to change. Descending slowly through the cloud came, first, the capsule, then the immense shape of the balloon. The cameraman leapt into action to capture the scene, and the angst of the previous few hours immediately became worth it. I'd got the story.

I often found that what I regarded as a normal day would be viewed by most as a long way from that description. But even I have to admit that events took a very strange turn next. From seemingly out of nowhere an aeroplane appeared and began to circle us as we filmed the balloon. It was a small four-seat single engine aircraft, much like the ones I flew. But what made this one stand out was that it was towing a long banner behind it. Quite what its purpose was in this bit of airspace I never discovered. I don't know whether it was an advertising stunt, with someone cashing in on the attention Branson's balloon was bound to get, or some social or political message aimed at Branson himself. I didn't manage to read what was on the banner, or if I did I don't remember the slogan, but it continued to circle us, and John, our pilot, was becoming alarmed. He regarded the potential for disaster as higher than he was prepared to accept. Also, our fuel reserves would soon become an issue. The twenty minutes of flying time we'd wasted because of the office's indecision and lack of good judgment had cost us dearly, and robbed me of options. I reluctantly agreed that we would leave the area, get some fuel, and decide what to do next. So we headed for Belfast.

There are two Belfast airports, Belfast Harbour, which is a city airport, and Belfast International, nearly fifteen miles to the west. We headed for the former, and soon were passing over the houses of the city below. I sensed the helicopter was flying faster, and asked if I was right. John's reply was surprising, and a little disconcerting. This was during the height of the Troubles, and he explained we were flying over Belfast in a type of helicopter which was used by the British Army. Those on the ground, he said, would have no indication that it was no longer military, and there were regular occurrences of Gazelles being fired at with rifles. I didn't much like the sound of that, and snuggled lower in my seat. Before long we were safely on the ground, having survived any bullets which had come our way. We quickly discovered John had made the wrong choice. There was industrial action that day at Belfast

Harbour, so no fuel was being pumped. I quickly arranged for a taxi to take the pictures we'd shot to the local ITV station so they could be transmitted back to our newsroom and onwards to ITN, ITV's national news service. Our only option now was the sprawling international airport close to Lough Neagh to the west. It was a short hop there, and as I stood alongside the helicopter on the huge apron talking on my phone, I became aware of someone taking up position close by. I looked around to find a policeman carrying a very large gun. I shouldn't have been surprised. Although it was rare in those days to see armed police at most UK airports, it seemed reasonable that they should be here on the ground in Northern Ireland. I did wonder whether he was here to protect me from the local population, or the local population from me. In the end I decided it was more likely the latter. I smiled at him. He didn't smile back.

We headed north, anxious to catch up on unfolding events. Air Traffic Control was helpful again, and as we approached Rathlin Island off the north coast I could see the massive balloon, partially collapsed in the water. It turned out that the capsule had hit the ground near Limavady, at which point two gas canisters had separated. The resultant loss of weight saw the balloon soar skywards. On its next descent it hit the water, and as it dragged along the surface, the Irish Sea began pouring into the capsule. The two occupants clambered onto the roof, and when it began to ascend again, Per Lindstrand leapt off from about sixty feet. He wasn't wearing a lifejacket. It was clear the aircraft was out of control, and the sole remaining occupant, Richard Branson, donned an oxygen mask and prepared to parachute to safety. But something made him delay, and as the balloon descended lower yet again he finally copied Per Lindstrand's actions and leapt into the sea.

Somewhere in the midst of this drama, I arrived back on the scene. A frantic search was underway to find the two adventurers and pluck them from their separate locations in the cold waters. We set down in a wheat field on Rathlin Island, next to what may well have been the sole phone box in this part of the world. My trusty mobile phone had no service here, so I called the newsroom from the box and reported progress into the nightly news programme, relating the adventure we'd been on and the current state of play. While I was doing this, John was negotiating with the farmer who'd turned up to complain about a small circle of wheat we'd flattened. It turned out to be worth £25. Before I hung up from my report, I was told that Channel 4 News wanted to speak with me, and at the top of their programme I reported the latest progress. By then, Richard Branson had been retrieved from the water by one of the rescue helicopters, but the search was still going on for Per Lindstrand. By now he'd been missing approaching two hours. I was asked to stay on the line, since they wanted to come back to me near the end of the programme. As I waited, John was monitoring the helicopter's radio a few feet away, and regularly arrived with another update. Eventually, Channel 4 News put me back on air, and just as I had begun answering their first question our pilot reappeared and whispered to me that Per Lindstrand had been found, and was well. I immediately broke the news to the nation, and heard my newsflash greeted by a huge cheer in the background. The programme was coming from the balloon flight's control room, and the news that Lindstrand was safe was greeted with an understandable wave of relief from everyone there. It was an emotional moment, and a fitting conclusion to the day. All that then remained for us to do was get ourselves home, so we clambered back into the helicopter for a final time, and taking care not to cause any more damage to the farmer's valuable crop, turned the nose eastwards.

The flight back was unremarkable. The adrenaline had stopped running in all of us, and tiredness was setting in. As we approached Carlisle, John was kind to me. Rather than heading directly to the airport, he dropped me off in the car park, which by now was almost deserted. I watched him depart with a wave as he got airborne again for the three minute flight to the airport, before going up to the newsroom. I felt the adventure had gone well, and idly imagined there might be a celebration under way. There wasn't. Instead, the lights were dim and the place was empty. If I'd had any thoughts of hearing the sound of champagne corks popping, I should have known better. The experience reinforced my understanding of the difference between the office workers and the road warriors. But on the plus side, it also saved me having an argument about the phone call to bring us home.

The following day I spent most of my time putting together a full report for that night's programme. Once that was complete I packed up my memories, put them away in the folder in my brain marked 'Done', and moved on.

THE AMERICAN DREAM

My first trip to the United States was a little bizarre. Its purpose was to film the delivery of a side of smoked salmon to a deli on Broadway in New York. The background to the story lay in a challenge I'd been set. Working at the smallest of Britain's ITV stations brought both advantages and drawbacks. The downside was that resources and equipment were in short supply. There weren't many people around, and the company couldn't afford the latest and shiniest kit. I had to make the best of what we had. However, we had recently bought an outside broadcast vehicle and its deployment one particular weekend created a dilemma. For all sorts of reasons, mainly involving agreements with the technicians' union, it wasn't going to be possible to fully populate the studio crew the day before the outside broadcast was due to take place. It meant that, on the face of it, broadcasting that evening's news programme was going to be impossible. However, someone came up with a clever wheeze to solve the problem. We'd produce a news bulletin to occupy the first ten minutes or so of the programme, which would be presented from a small continuity studio. This was almost a cupboard where the links between programmes came from, and crucially didn't need a cast of thousands to operate. The rest of the programme would be composed of a single film of about fifteen minutes. Now, coming up with the technical solution was one thing. Making a suitable film was another. So I was summoned and told to conceive a plan.

A few weeks earlier I'd been shooting a news story at a local company which produced seafood. In conversation with the managing director he'd told me that they were very successful in the export market, and mentioned that a side of smoked salmon was sent each week to Zabar's, a high class deli on Broadway at 80th Street in New York. Wouldn't it be interesting, I thought, now that we've seen where the salmon comes from, to explore where it goes. It was an unusual story for a highly unusual situation. But there was a good editorial reasoning behind it, and its relatively spectacular nature would provide a smokescreen around a slightly embarrassing problem.

I've found that having the creative idea is usually relatively easy. Turning the idea into watchable television is plain hard work. And before you even shoot the first foot of film, the logistics of the operation must be carefully analysed and organised. That, in particular, was the part of programme making that some of my colleagues ddn't understand. Over the years they saw me travelling overseas on shoots, and equated getting on an aeroplane with going on holiday. I couldn't really blame them, since that was how their lives were arranged. But I never figured out why they would be jealous of long flights, jet-lag, noisy motels, long drives, lack of sleep, and constant, constant exhaustion. Once or twice I took a different crew with me on these trips. It was inevitably a nightmare, and they rarely wanted to come again. But I prided myself on my organisational skills. Everything, down to the smallest detail, was planned meticulously, and it was extremely rare for anything to go wrong.

My first call was to the seafood company. Foremost amongst the long list of things I needed if the film was to happen was the side of salmon. Without it, there wouldn't be any point in going all the way to New York. When I explained the plan to the seafood company's managing director he was immediately enthusiastic, and happy to commit to letting me have the salmon to take to one of his most important overseas customers. It would be excellent PR for him, both here and there. I put the first tick on my checklist.

It's worth pointing out at this stage that the technical side of the company wasn't the only area which was, of necessity, denuded of resources. I once took the final programme of a small business series to California so that the winners from the regional heats could be inspired by how American entrepreneurs operated similar businesses to their own. The producer of the previous series had organised a slap-up dinner in a local hotel for the finalists. Although it had worked well, I wanted to give them food for thought instead, a stimulation which would help their businesses grow. We'd been there for a week when the judges flew in. I had reached my, by now, regular state of exhaustion, and when one particular judge, who was a high ranking manager in a very large international company based in our region, hadn't arrived at the hotel by midnight, I went off and collapsed into bed. An hour later I was awoken by a phone call. The missing judge had arrived very angry, and was demanding to see me. I got dressed and went down to reception so he could have someone to shout at. The guy was a nervous flyer, I decided, and he'd been spooked by being on the last plane to get out of Boston's Logan Airport before it was shut down by a snowstorm. By all accounts it had been a hairy take-off. But what was much worse, and had been the main trigger for the temper tantrum, was that the flight had been full, so he hadn't been upgraded to business class. The fact that he was standing in a fine hotel next to the Universal Studio lot in Hollywood counted for nothing. He was upset because he'd had to travel in coach. I waited patiently for the tidal wave to subside, and just before it did, he delivered his coup de grâce. "If you were working for me," he thundered, "I would have you and the entire team who organised this fiasco sacked." As his words echoed off into the distance, his spittle settled on the hotel's luxurious carpet, and the reception staff pretended they were elsewhere, something happened which he was entirely unprepared for. I smiled. I actually nearly laughed, but that would have been rude. Very softly I said to him, "There is no team to sack. There are no backroom staff who've spent their days and weeks organising this. The combined total of employees who've been involved in putting this together is standing before you now. Me." And it was true. Much later in my programme making, I would occasionally be able to afford a researcher to help out. But for most of the time, for most of the programmes, it was me and me alone. And I was glad. Because I had learned very early on of the imperative of making sure that I sought out all of the potential pitfalls and laid in contingency plans before going on a shoot. If I didn't, and things fell apart, there was only me on hand to put it back together again. So best get it right first time. The judge was used to an operation where the assistants had assistants, so this was confusing territory. I took him for a drink before I headed back to bed. I don't know whether he came to respect what I was trying to do, but we got on well from then on.

Throughout my career I was constantly inventing ways of doing things for a cost that was somewhere between cheap and free, relying on the people I was asking for help to see some advantage in being involved. This even extended to my cameraman, Eric, and his sound recordist, Allan. They gave a huge amount of their time freely to make the programmes I wanted to make, gaining nothing more than an interesting experience and a stretching of the mind in return. Without their help and understanding I couldn't have achieved what I did, and for that I am deeply in their debt. But conversely, they had a collection of experiences that few others could match. And in my book, at least, that made up for any slight inconveniences.

With the salmon now promised, I was faced with organising how to get it to its destination. The first part of the trip was easy. The second turned out to be a very close run thing. I had good connections with the local airport at the time, and knew the marketing team at the airline which was operating flights to London, having covered the inauguration of their service a few months previously. I called Annette, their marketing manager, and she immediately offered to take us and the salmon to and from London. But how would I get from there to New York? I tried my luck with British Airways, reasoning that the national carrier would be most likely to see a value in being involved. They listened to me, and although they didn't sound hugely enthusiastic, agreed to make the case for us and promised to call back. Time was very tight, and there wasn't much leeway in my schedule. The programme my film was needed for was on the Friday of the following week. That meant that I would have to make the journey within the next seven days, and the timescale was complicated by the presence of a Bank Holiday the following Monday. If we were to go on the Tuesday morning, I'd have the remainder of that day and part of Wednesday to film in New York. I'd catch the overnight flight back on Wednesday night and have Thursday and Friday to edit it. It was tight, but doable. However, most crucially, the last day I'd have available to persuade people to help us would be the end of the week, and that was approaching quickly. While I awaited a response from British Airways I began to put together the remaining pieces of the jigsaw. I organised a driver and a crew vehicle in New York, reasoning that it was an unnecessary additional pressure to do the driving and navigation ourselves. He agreed to collect us at the airport. I'm not sure how I chose the hotel. It was a bit of a lottery, and it wasn't my best decision. It turned out to be just a few yards from the local fire station, and I ended up being woken several times during the night by the noise of sirens as the engines went off to save lives and douse flames.

There were also two important paperwork issues to be dealt with. One involved acquiring a carnet. This is a formal document which is required by customs officials, and enabled us to export our equipment from the UK, temporarily import it into the United States, and then do the same in reverse on the return journey. It's vital that the information it contains is completely accurate. Failure to ensure this can lead to some very expensive property being seized. There was one trip where a cameraman decided he'd be smart with customs and it backfired dramatically. On his return to the UK he was quizzed about whether he'd brought back exactly what he'd taken away. In his notoriously condescending way he looked down his nose at the customs officer and explained that, when he'd taken the film out of the country it was unexposed. However, since he'd obviously used it for filming it was now exposed. His imperious attempt at a putdown wasn't appreciated, and the film was promptly impounded. I felt it would be good if that didn't happen to me. Jeanette, the Financial Director's very able and highly efficient secretary, took responsibility for the carnet. The remaining requirement was for a visa which would allow us to enter the United States for the purposes of work. I discovered we could get one from the US Consulate in Edinburgh. I knew the place well, since the building was situated in between those of my old school. I had suffered double Latin first thing on a Monday morning next door, so it wasn't a place I could easily forget. The three of us duly made the trip to the Scottish capital to hand over some money and collect the necessary stamp in our passports. And on the way back I called in to pick up the real star of the show, the box of salmon.

As the week progressed alarmingly quickly I kept in contact with British Airways and continued to hear reassuring noises. I didn't really have a Plan B, so I was relying on them coming up trumps. The cost of paying for three sets of return tickets was just too much for the programme budget to bear. But unbeknown to me, the film sound recordist who'd been assigned to the job, one of only two employed by the company, was involved in his own calculations. He had planned to go away for a few days with his wife, and was faced with a predicament. Did he have enough faith in my abilities to make the filming trip happen, thus meaning he'd have to cancel his break, or was he tempting fate by believing in me, and thereby courting trouble with his wife if I failed? It was a close-run decision, but ultimately he chose the wrong option. He stuck with the holiday.

During Friday I called British Airways several times, but still couldn't get a commitment from them. At just before five o'clock, ahead of the Bank Holiday weekend, I rolled the dice a final time. It took a lot of persuasion, but finally we had an agreement. The tickets would be available for us on departure. I spread the news that the shoot was definitely on, and was met with the sound recordist's confession that he now couldn't go. It was a hammer blow. All it had needed was for one brick in the wall to crack and the whole carefully constructed plan looked in danger of falling apart. The sound recordist's ill-judged decision seemed have scuppered things. But then I remembered that the company's other film crew had been to the US before. Did its sound recordist still have a valid visa? The answer to my question of Cliff was an emphatic *Yes*, delivered with a beaming smile. And so it came to pass that we were, at last, ready for our epic journey to begin the following Tuesday at 7 am.

My first visit to The Big Apple was interesting, if short. And because I would only be there for about thirty hours, I knew I had to be very efficient. Immigration checks at John F Kennedy Airport went without a hitch, our shiny new visas being accepted without a murmur. Customs was a little more time consuming, with the agent checking serial numbers on some items of equipment to be satisfied that the carnet was accurate. But finally he stamped it, tore off his own copy and waved us on our way. He appeared not to notice, or be concerned about, the box of smoked salmon I was carrying under my arm. As I emerged from the terminal building it seemed I had entered Bedlam. The scene before me was one of utter chaos as hundreds of people fought for taxis, cars, rental buses and nearly every form of transport you could imagine. The roadway was a massive traffic jam, with drivers stopping at random to pick up their rides. I began to scan the vehicles, looking for one that matched the description I'd been given for ours. And there it was, a couple of hundred yards away, parked on the opposite kerb. The driver was alert, which was a good start, and saw me waving at him. Although it was going to be difficult either way, since we had two heavy trolleys loaded with bags and equipment, it seemed more sensible for him to fight his way through the melee rather than us push our loads the other way. After five minutes or so he'd managed to get half way to us, but it was clear he wasn't going to make it further without some form of intervention. So I strode into the road and began directing traffic, banging on roofs and bonnets and urging the drivers of the vehicles to bring a sense of order to proceedings by moving aside. There wasn't any kickback, just an acceptance that this guy knew something they didn't. Grudgingly, they made some small effort to comply. It was my first lesson in New York life, and although I can't say I ever became particularly expert, I did manage to make my way. The key, it seemed, was to become larger than life. I decided it wasn't too far removed from how things were back home. It was just that the world here was bigger, louder, more populous and far more aggressive. But I was up for that.

The driver, Joe, was friendly. And quite rightly so. I would be paying hm a lot of money to ferry us around. As he extricated us from the chaos of the airport and navigated into the larger chaos of the Van Wyck Expressway, I began to see road signs for some of the iconic names I'd heard about from movies - Queens, Manhattan, The Bronx - and it suddenly became real. A helicopter buzzed low and fast overhead, carrying passengers who'd just arrived on flights like ours to the city ahead. Below, the traffic around gently carried us forward, like a boat on a slow moving river. I watched the helicopter disappear into the distance with a sense of envy. As we crawled along I spoke with Joe. He did a lot of work with film crews, so he knew the way we'd operate. Most importantly, not only did he know his way around this huge, confusing and potentially dangerous city, he'd also prove very helpful in suggesting locations which matched the sort of images I wanted to grab. My idea was to film the completion of our journey by delivering the salmon to Zabar's Deli, before constructing the remainder of the item as a colour piece which gave a flavour of New York.

I can't honestly say how long it took to get from JFK to Broadway, but it felt like a couple of hours. We pulled up close to Zabar's and Joe said he'd guard the vehicle and equipment while we worked. That was a reassuring role I'd come to miss on later visits for reasons of cost. I entered what seemed like a very ordinary looking deli and introduced myself to the manager, explaining what we were doing and what I needed from him. He took it in his stride and we were done in half an hour or so. I was dismayed to see that, as soon as we finished, the box of salmon I'd carefully carried the three and a half thousand miles from home was casually discarded in the bin. The manager noticed my look. "Can't sell it now," he said simply. "It's been too warm for too long."

By now it was the time of the evening commute and the light was starting to fade, so I asked Joe to take us to our hotel and arranged a time for him to collect us in the morning. He went cheerily on his way and we entered our home for the night. It was a run of the mill hotel - probably mid to low end - and I had the sense to ask the receptionist for some local advice. He suggested somewhere across the road to eat, and warned us to be off the streets before the theatre-goers melted away. His final message was a lot closer to home. "Don't open your door to anyone through the night," he said. I wondered about a hotel which had bad guys wandering the corridors, but didn't raise it with him. We all exchanged looks as we absorbed the information and headed for the lift. It was pretty much a case of dumping our bags and equipment in the rooms and heading out to eat. Our bodies were telling us that it was five hours later than the clocks read. We were ravenous and we were tired. Since setting off that morning we'd had two airline meals and a snack. I sensed there was a steak nearby with my name on it.

The effect of westward transatlantic travel was one I'd get used to and enjoy over the years ahead. On this trip we were only crossing five time zones, and with our exposure to the change being so short, it would barely affect us on our return home, but it did mean that I could expect to be up early the following morning. I closed the hotel room door for the night, carefully applying all of the additional locks for safety, and sneaked a look through the spy hole lest an axe murderer had followed me. I didn't want to be awoken by a voice in the night calling, "Here's Johnny!" The clock by the bedside showed 9 pm. My body laughed. It knew the time was really 2 am, and it was ready to switch off - perhaps anxious was a better description - and sleep came quickly.

It was a crisp winter's day, with a clear sky and the merest breath of wind rustling the remaining leaves not yet shed by the ancient oaks standing guard around the lake. In another week or two the ice would form, sealing the surface with an impenetrable translucent crust until the arrival of regeneration the following Spring. But this morning the water was still in liquid form, its surface an unblemished mirror reflecting the subtle graduation of blue above. The day was sharp with frost, my breath casting a vapour trail, my feet softly breaking the silence, each step marked by a gentle breakfast-cereal crunch. I was grateful for the down jacket, gloves and hat I'd been lent by my host to keep me warm, and I felt myself instinctively snuggling deeper into their protective layers. There was a tranquility about the scene that was somehow reassuring. I felt as if I belonged here. The parallax of trees and background smoothly altered as I moved, mimicking the view of a Steadicam tracking across a movie set. My mind was as relaxed as my body, floating in a world where gravity exerted no pull. Calm. Serene. From my left, disconnected and distant, came the softest hint of sound. Enough to create awareness, but not yet sufficiently intrusive to cause irritation, to interfere with the perfection of the day. As time continued its slow-motion progress, the noise began to resolve itself, slowly emerging from a confusion of silence to become identifiable as the friendly honking of a far-off goose calling to a kindred spirit. I could imagine its feathers caressing the air around, parting it, extracting energy for flight, the graceful motion leaving behind the gentlest swish of vortices as the only evidence the bird had ever been there. I slowly grew aware of a question forming deep within my soul. The call of the goose became more strident, and I began to feel the moment slipping from my grasp. Before it broke I remember thinking about whether birds suffer from laryngitis. And then I was awake, panicking in the darkness of my unfamiliar surroundings, still hearing the noise of the goose from my dream, only closer, louder, more rasping. Reality stepped up and regained control, and I lay there cursing as the first departing fire engine was joined by a second, their bright plumage illuminated by red and blue flashing strobes reflecting through the window as they transported their own miniature lakes to douse the flames of someone's misfortune. I looked across at the red segments on the LED clock display. 3:18. I carried out a swift calculation and realised it was 8:18 at home. My night's sleep was over. At 5 am I gave up any further pretence and rose, thankful that I'd arranged to meet the others early at seven for breakfast. In reality, my body thought that breakfast was lunch, and that made the experience even more indulgent and enjoyable.

We picked our way through the morning traffic and crossed the street once more, heading for what I imagined was a typical New York breakfast joint. I wasn't disappointed, even if only by the greeting. We took a table and coffee arrived almost instantly, accompanied by an aggressive "What d'ya want?" I wasn't sure of the protocol, but took a chance and smiled at the server. The charm offensive was quickly rebuffed by an impatient look which spoke volumes, one of which was entitled *Why Am I Still Standing Here*? I ordered New York strip steak and eggs, determined to get the most from this culinary experience. I sensed that more was expected of me, but before I could collect my wits I found myself on the receiving end of another verbal barrage. "Hash browns? What kinda toast? How d'ya want the eggs?" It all seemed very complicated for an outsider, and I felt little sense that I was about the be given a gentle lesson on the art of ordering the American Way. It was a harsh introduction, perhaps, but I came to love breakfast in America. Hell, Supertramp even wrote a song about it. I can only guess at how many times across subsequent years I sat down in Denny's to order breakfast. Certainly more than one hundred, maybe less than two. After a long while I tired of my amateurish approach to this clearly serious business, and worked hard to tick every available option, relieving the server of the tiresome need to ask this foreigner to clarify the final request on the road to perfection. I confess with a certain embarrassment that I could count on one hand the times I actually succeeded. But it was all part of the theatre. The steak and eggs that morning were delicious, and the coffee just kept on coming.

Suitably wired with the help of more caffeine than I would normally consume in a week, we walked back to the hotel to collect our bags and equipment, and to say goodbye to the same receptionist who'd greeted us the night before. It seemed odd to have travelled so far for half a night's sleep. Yet here we were, already starting the journey home. Before we made it back to the door of the aircraft I needed to film the rest of the material required to put the programme together, and as we carried our gear out to Joe and the waiting van I realised I only had a hazy idea of what I wanted to do. I had some flexibility over timing, with a promise that the length of the news bulletin would be adjusted to compensate for the length of my film. It wouldn't have to be a precise duration, but I'd be expected to turn in something that was in the region of fifteen minutes. I quickly discussed some options with Joe, and began to formulate a more considered approach to the day. It would evolve over time, but I knew where we'd start - Wall Street. The world's financial centre. As Joe drove expertly through the traffic, I asked the cameraman to film along the way, capturing the bustle of life in the metropolis. We didn't exactly see The Village People, but all of the New York bit players were there, and we hoovered them up like tourists.

Wall Street was an eye-opener. I decided to carry out some vox-pop, sampling the voice of the people. I hated it generally. When the news desk couldn't think of a story to cover we'd be sent to do vox pop, to ask the man and woman in the street what they thought of a particular semi-newsworthy topic. Even in a quiet, relaxed area like the one we covered, people were often too busy to be bothered to stop and answer what they regarded as stupid questions. I would soon discover that, on Wall Street, it was an order of magnitude harder. We were working with a true film camera, and we used a hybrid system for sound, sometimes recording onto a magnetic stripe on the film, sometimes on a separate recorder. For our vox pop we'd use the first method, which necessitated the sound recordist being attached to the camera by an umbilical cord. As it turned out, that would be extremely useful. My first victim approached and I set to work. As he strode towards me I greeted him confidently and politely. "Good morning sir. British television." Without breaking step or wasting his time with even a glance he snarled a guttural reply, "I don't talk to British television," and swept past. OK. That had gone well. I tried half a dozen others, receiving a variety of similar responses, none positive. Today's reporters work with cameras that record on tape or memory cards. They're cheap and re-usable. Film was expensive, had a one-time use, and importantly, a magazine held just ten minutes of footage. I'd just burned through a couple of minutes of film with nothing to show for it. But I always try to be a quick learner, so I adopted a new strategy. I ramped up the aggression level to one which seemed commensurate with that employed by our server at breakfast, and I taught the crew how to play the part of a roadblock. The sound recordist stood against the wall of the merchant bank we happened to be outside. The cameraman stood four feet out from the wall with the cable running between them, and I positioned myself a couple of feet in front. Together we created three sides of a box from which there was no escape. All I had to do was funnel people into the box. It worked like a charm. Trapped by our configuration, and faced with a by-now very insistent inquisitor, everyone acquiesced. Within a few minutes we were done. I'd learned a valuable lesson, and I'd completed another of the segments I needed.

From there on the day went well. I set about the remainder of my tasks with new found vigour, adapting and evolving as we continued to make progress, each piece of a jigsaw slotting into place in my head. Many years later someone said to me that she couldn't understand how I kept all of the elements of a six part series in my memory at the same time, remembering everything down to individual shots. I didn't regard it as any special gift or skill. I'm sure that every programme maker has to do something similar. What it made me suspect was that she didn't involve herself enough in the filming process, preferring to abdicate responsibility to the cameraman alone. The visual memory is well equipped to store information. But if you don't direct the shots, if you're not there to collect the memories, even the most efficient storage system will be unable to recall them.

All too soon our time was up. There's always a feeling that you need a little bit more, just one additional shot. But at some point you have to draw a line. And in this instance it involved ensuring we made it back to the aircraft which would take us home. Joe took us to JFK and I felt he'd been incredibly good value as I handed over his payment. I knew I couldn't have managed it without him. And as we boarded the aircraft I was already analysing my performance on the shoot and the decisions I'd made, in a self de-brief that has continued after every shoot to this day. It had gone well, and I could add another interesting experience to my list. The lights of New York disappeared behind the clouds as we climbed out on departure, and I settled down for the overnight flight home. Hopefully, I'd manage to get some sleep on the way back. One thing was for sure. It wouldn't be interrupted by any fire engines.

By the time I got back to editing I had less than two days before transmission. My cameraman, previously an editor, had once famously said to his boss, "Everyone knows you can only edit five minutes of airtime a day." "No," came the response. "Everyone knows *you* can only edit five minutes of airtime a day." But he had a point. I had less than two days to create at least fifteen minutes of television. It was going to be interesting. If I failed, the screen would be black.

Perhaps before I go further, this is the moment for another confession. I had been aware for a few days that sometime around now there was going to be the mother of all arguments, and it was entirely my fault. To understand why, we need to examine the working practices of those dim and distant days before electronic video cameras and computer editing. It was a Heath Robinson affair which relied more upon mechanical engineering than its electronic equivalent. Film is a physical medium. Once it's been developed you can hold it up to the light and see the pictures. Editing the type of film we used was a destructive process. You physically cut it into the lengths you needed, joined them together with transparent sticky tape, and the result was what was shown on screen. One of the many drawbacks of this approach was that you were limited to cuts between shots. If we wanted a dissolve we had to run two separate film tracks in synchronisation on two different telecine machines. Then there was the sound. The film stock we used had a soundtrack attached, a magnetic stripe which ran along the edge of the celluloid. But we also employed a technique where sound was recorded onto a separate recorder. At its most complex we could have two picture tracks and four sound tracks running, all synchronised together. The editors were highly skilled at what they did, and their biggest fear was losing sync between the multiple tracks. It was a potential nightmare.

The problem I had created centred on the very strict instructions I'd been given prior to the shoot, that I could only have one film track with its associated, attached audio. Because the programme was being originated from the presentation studio, the facilities for mixing sound and vision were not available. It meant that the film would have to be unrealistically basic. I couldn't, for example, use any music. But there were many other limitations, and I knew they'd be very obvious to the viewer. So I decided early on in the production that I'd simply ignore what I'd been told and make the film the way it should be made. I couldn't see why the viewers should get a sub-standard product, so as someone much wiser than me explained it many years later, I had tossed a pebble in the pond and was waiting to see where the ripples went. When they hit the shore they caused a little unpleasantness, but a good natured technician agreed to a bit of overtime so he could operate the studio's mixing console, allowing the film could go out the way I intended.

It had seemed an impossible task, but I had managed to bring all of the elements together in a remarkably short time to produce an interesting film which put the export work of a local company in context. It had also met a need, whilst dealing with the regular problem of not having enough people to do the necessary jobs. I'd learned a lot from the experience. Foremost was a challenge to the belief that staff numbers presented a road block. I'd shown that we could reach beyond the possible to achieve something which lifted us above the mundane, using a little ingenuity, mixed with determination and a lot of hard work. It began to form a template in my mind which would be the foundation upon which I would build many similar, but far more ambitious projects in the future.

DARK DAYS

One of the more enjoyable parts of my job has been the freedom it has given me to drop into someone's world for a few hours and learn a bit about them. It's provided an insight into the breadth of life experiences people have, and how each of us lives a different normality, which in turn creates a unique perspective on life. The reasons which would bring me into contact with an individual varied enormously. In my time as a programme maker it would invariably come about through my choosing. The person would possess a skill or knowledge which was important for me to call upon in telling a story. However, as a news reporter, happenstance would more often be a driver, as I chased the outcomes of everyday events to report their effects on those they touched. Most usually, the impact of such reporting on me would be minimal, and I had observed with some fascination, as if from a distance, the methods I had evolved to allow me to deal with the pressures of the job. To many it might have seemed cold-hearted. In the acquisition phase during filming, I would absorb events with little time for analysis or emotional response. The focus was largely on watching and recording situations. Only later, once the acquisition was complete, would I move to the second phase of trying to make sense of what I'd seen, and to understand its importance. The American publisher Philip Graham described news as a first draft of history, and it was important to ensure that the pace of reporting was not responsible for a misrepresentation of perspective. The advent of 24 hour rolling news made this burden an order of magnitude harder, and continues to put an unfair pressure on journalists to know more than is possible in providing instant analysis of sometimes cataclysmic events.

I saw an example of this on September 11th 2001. I had been drawn to one of the televisions in the newsroom when the first reports of Amercan Airlines Flight 11 hitting the World Trade Center's North Tower made it to air. Seventeen minutes after that first aircraft crashed, United Airlines Flight 175 struck the South Tower. In the pressure cooker atmosphere of a live television studio, one presenter struggled to make sense of what had just appeared on our screens. Unable to comprehend the scale of the terror attack, she described it as an awful coincidence. Watching the progress of events through a television screen has a sanitising effect, whether we see it as a viewer or a commentator. Being there on the ground takes the experience to a different level, and the reality can be painful. There were two instances when my well-practised techniques failed me completely, and watching as events unfolded left a scar which remains to this day.

The first was in 1982 when I attended the funeral of an eleven year old girl, Susan Maxwell. Susan had been abducted while walking home over the bridge across the River Tweed between Coldstream and Cornhill-on-Tweed after a tennis game with her friend. Her body was discovered weeks later in a ditch close to a lay-by near Uttoxeter, more than 250 miles away. I had been aware of the story, but hadn't been involved in any of its reporting. However, the day before her funeral was due to take place I was assigned to cover it. Late that morning, I did something I would find difficult to do today. Back then I suppose I was something of an innocent. It wasn't that I was in any way callous about the anguish her parents must have been going through. Rather, I'd never suffered much in the way of tragedy in my life, and the effect it had on the lives of those it touched was beyond my understanding. So I picked up the phone and asked Susan's mother, Liz, if I could interview her. Liz was a journalist, so she understood how powerful the interview would be, and the possible benefit the publicity could provide for the police investigation. But I remember her saying to me that she couldn't do an interview on the day she buried her daughter. If I wanted one, it would have to be that afternoon. It was a very reasonable response to what many would have regarded as an unreasonable request. The logistics of carrying out the interview that afternoon, followed by the coverage of the funeral the following day, meant the crew and I would have to overnight, probably in Coldstream. So I told Liz I'd get an agreement for that and call her back. The next few hours were an eye-opener for me.

For reasons you'll come to understand, I'll anonymise the next part of events. At this time there was a culture of heavy drinking within the company, symptomatic of a general approach to journalism which would often uncover its stories in smoke-filled bars. Alcohol was an important part of the working day for some people, and there was a small number of pubs that various of our managers and others would congregate in to socialise, both during and after work. The person from whom I needed authority to spend the money involved in an overnight was a member of this group, and it didn't present a difficult challenge for me to guess which watering hole I would find him in. I got it right on the first attempt. Let's, for the sake of simplicity, call him John. It was shortly before midday when I got him on the phone and explained the situation. If I'd been expecting a decision there and then I was to be disappointed. Instead he said to me, "I'll come back and sort it out." I suppose I've always been guilty of imagining that the story I'm working on is the most significant, but it's an opinion that's probably hard-wired into most journalists. I naturally expected *come back and sort it out* actually meant *come back and sort it out now*. But I was severely overestimating the importance of the interview to John, and equally miscalculating the pull of the pint. So I sat in the newsroom and watched the clock tick by with a barely concealed frustration. I didn't count each one individually, but the clock ticked twelve thousand times before John reappeared. And then I discovered what the phrase *sort it out* really meant.

There can be few occasions when I've felt as ashamed of my job as I did over the next few minutes. I don't know how much lager had been consumed, and can't be sure that it actually played a part in events, but such was the appalling lack of judgment he displayed that I can only assume it must have been responsible. He dialled the number I gave him, and in a moment he was speaking to Liz. John's desk was behind mine, and as the conversation progressed I knew I couldn't trust myself to turn round. I heard him tell the woman who had agreed to face a television camera the day before she buried her young daughter that an overnight stay would be too expensive. He explained we could only do the interview the following morning, ahead of the ceremony. It was condescending in the extreme, and thoughtless beyond measure. In the end, Liz put the phone down on him. I felt like doing something far more dramatic, but by that point it wouldn't have solved anything. There was no embarrassment in his voice when he told me the interview was off.

The following day I set off with the crew for the journey north. It was a drive of nearly two hours through the A-roads of the Scottish borders. For an event like this I always wanted to be early, and we arrived with plenty of time to spare. Cornhill is a beautiful, quiet village close to the River Tweed, which at that point forms the boundary between Scotland and England. The area is heavy on historical importance. Cornhill's population is in the low hundreds, but that day it was busy. Such was the expected show of sympathy at the funeral that a speaker system had been set up in the open air to allow the overflow congregation to hear the service and participate. This was a close-knit community. I needed to recce the situation and understand what lay ahead. The first port of call was St Helen's Church to track down the vicar. On the way in I noticed a bench where parishioners could sit and contemplate the events which had led them to this spot. It was new, and on the back was a shiny brass plate with an inscription. It showed that the bench had been gifted in memory of Susan by the local newspaper. The vicar was very helpful and understanding. He appreciated the sensitivity of the situation as much as I did, but wanted to do what he could to help. He told me where the burial would take place, in the annexe churchyard a few yards away behind the village hall. I walked the route the tiny coffin would soon take, and found myself in a peaceful corner of the village which provided privacy for those who came to visit their loved ones. I decided where we would need to be, positioned a discrete distance from the ceremony, but still able to observe events.

It wasn't unusual to feel detached from what we were filming. It was a rare day that we would discuss how we felt about something we'd seen. We just tried to get on with our jobs and do what had to be done. Only this day was different. When the church service concluded we followed the small procession to the churchyard, filming as we went, and watched as the coffin was lowered into the grave. Just before she turned and walked away, Liz dropped something onto it. Instinctively, I knew it was important, so I waited until the area was quieter before walking to the graveside. I called the cameraman over and asked for a shot of what I'd seen. There, lying on top of the casket, was a single red rose, and with it a note. It said simply, "Sorry I missed you". I looked around for our electrician, and saw he had moved to the south east corner of the churchyard. His shoulders were softly heaving, the only indication from a distance that he was crying. Gordon had two daughters, and was better able than the rest of us to empathise with the family's pain. I don't know if any of the others had noticed the scene, but it was never spoken of.

The journey back was frustrating. We departed behind the police car containing a detective from Staffordshire who'd travelled north for the funeral. He had a longer trip ahead of him than we had, but I felt the greater sense of urgency. In those days we shot on film. It was long before the advent of electronic cameras for news gathering. This meant the film had to be processed before I could begin work with an editor to put the story together. We were all lost in our thoughts, wrapped up in what we'd been a part of. I began to write my script, occasionally glancing up at the road ahead, as if searching for inspiration. Always, there was the police car, a moving road block impeding our progress and slowing us down. It was obvious that the driver was balancing a desire to move as quickly as possible with a concern for the comfort of his back seat passenger. Perhaps the detective was working, like me. Or maybe he didn't want to be made to feel uncomfortable on the twisty country roads. The result was that his driver would take bends unaccountably slowly, before accelerating on the straight stretches. His cornering speed was much slower than ours, and at each turn in the road we'd be sitting on his rear bumper, eager to pass. But just as we thought an opportunity was opening up, the police car would bound ahead, leaving us trailing in its wake. Its presence meant there would be a price to pay a few hours later.

There can't be too many of today's television journalists who have worked with film. It was an inflexible and unforgiving medium. It required great skill of a cameraman, who had to expose it with an accuracy foreign to today's shooters. The chemical process to develop it demanded an equal precision. And the editors who worked with me to create a finished package in a very short period of time were artists to be admired, cutting and splicing the acetate with a meticulous ease which belied the potential for disaster. The process was invasive, and for someone with less well-honed abilities, it was very easy to scratch or otherwise damage the pictures. Shooting the story was only the beginning. The processing and editing took a finite length of time, and we regularly pushed the limits of what was possible to try to get a late story on air. Today would be one such day, thanks to the care of a police driver.

Our programme went to air at 6 pm, and all of the prepared film stories were cut together on a giant reel in the order in which they would be shown. Occasionally a film hadn't finished being edited by the time this happened, and in these cases it would be loaded onto a reel of its own, to be played from a separate telecine machine, part film projector, part television scanner. Alongside the film was a roll of audio tape, the same size and with the same perforations, which would run in synchronisation with the pictures. It was a complicated set-up, a combining of electronics and mechanics. It took time to load the spools, threading the film and tape through a series of guides before the giant machine could be run. My report was the lead story that night, and it was late. When the edit was complete, I left the editor and the film assistant to finish off. There was nothing more I could do. Transmission was now only a few minutes away, and the crew ended up with me in the board room with a drink in hand to watch the report go out. It took me a long time to realise that a finished production would often be a surprise for the cameraman. Although they had filmed the constituent parts, often they could only guess at how it would all go together, and I felt it was important that they could see how their hard work panned out. Hopefully we would all learn lessons from what we saw, and improve the way we worked next time round. I saw this feedback loop as a vital part of my own journey of discovery, and couldn't understand those journalists and programme makers I observed over the years absolving themselves from the responsibilities of directing the cameraman or controlling the edit.

The drink was not a celebration. It wasn't that sort of day. Its purpose was to try to remove the razor sharp emotions we'd all endured, and help bond us in the common experience. I made it to a seat just as the programme's opening tiles cut to the studio presenter. He immediately launched into the script I'd written to introduce the item. Even as he read, a technician was scrambling to lace up the film and audio tape and get them synchronised. It was going to be a close run thing. The presenter concluded the introduction with, "This report from Ian Fisher," and looked down to his monitor. But nothing changed. The film didn't appear, and we continued to watch the presenter's face. Eventually, he broke lock with the monitor and began shuffling papers on the desk. A voice in his earpiece was passing instructions. But rather than explain there was a problem, and that we'd return to the report in a moment, he chose for some inexplicable reason to ignore it completely. The frustrations and tensions of the day exploded amongst our small boardroom group, and there was some very ungentlemanly abuse aimed at the screen. But a few minutes later the report did make it to air and the funeral of eleven year old Susan Maxwell was cemented in history. We had completed our task, and I prepared to tackle the next news story that would come my way, leaving the events of the day to fade into the clutter of life. But not quite.

The privilege my job afforded me of being able to intrude

into someone's life was only one side of the equation. What I hadn't given much thought to was how how these people continued once our paths had diverged. The events surrounding that fateful day have stayed with the Maxwell family since, colouring their lives with a permanent stain of tragedy. After the shameful way John had behaved on the phone, I considered offering an apology. But I came to the conclusion that they had enough to deal with, and that any further contact from me could only add to their pain. Perhaps, after all, it was only my own conscience I was attempting to assuage. I never did get an opportunity to speak with Liz again, but I regularly think about her and Susan. That day left an imprint in my non-volatile memory of life, a permanent scar brought about by a synchronicity no-one could have foreseen, when the lives of a little girl and a serial killer intersected on the bridge over the River Tweed. It was the first time Susan had been allowed to walk home by herself. Who could have known she would cross paths with a monster?

Twelve years later, on 19th May 1994, Robert Black, a van driver from Hoxton in London, originally from Grangemouth in Scotland, was convicted of Susan's murder. He had killed at least four children over a long period of time, and was suspected of being involved in the deaths of many others as far afield as Germany, The Netherlands, Ireland and France. Black was imprisoned for life, with a recommendation that he serve at least 35 years. He died in Maghaberry Prison in Northern Ireland on 12th January 2016 at the age of 68.

In a BBC studio in Glasgow at the very beginning of my broadcast career I found myself sitting opposite an exceptional man. Sammy Cahn was an American songwriter, four times winner of an Academy Award for his songs. He'd written some memorable lyrics for many of the great singers of his time, and worked extensively with Frank Sinatra. Songs such as *All the Way*, *Come Fly With Me*, *My Kind of Town* and *Three Coins in the Fountain* all flowed from his pen. I had a keen interest in songwriters, admiring their use of language to reflect emotion. Sammy had requested a typewriter be available, and as we sat waiting for the studio manager to turn up, he began working on a song. I was mesmerised by the creative process, and with a confidence way beyond my years, even offered some suggestions. In the subsequent interview I asked the inevitable question. "Which comes first? The words or the music?" The response was characteristically unexpected. In an acknowledgement that many of his songs were written at the request of movie producers for their latest production, he replied, "The phone call." Thus it was for me with Lockerbie.

Most people can recall where they were on 22nd November 1963. I was at a bus stop in Cluny Gardens, Edinburgh waiting for a number 39 bus. As I stood there, someone told me that the American President, John F. Kennedy, had been shot. Such was the importance of the event in world history that it's indelibly marked in our consciousness. I also know exactly where I was on 21st December 1988 when I first heard that an aircraft had fallen on the Scottish town of Lockerbie. It was the evening of the company's Christmas party, and I had come home to eat before returning for the festivities.

By now I had ceased to be a news reporter and presenter. I had been Programme Editor of the evening news programme, responsible for its day-to-day operation, before becoming a producer and director. However, despite having moved on from news coverage, when reports of the crash of an aircraft started coming in it was my phone that rang. It's plausible that there were two possible reasons I was asked to cover the story. It would be nice to think it was because of my knowledge of aviation, and an experience of covering multiple previous crashes. But it's also conceivable that anyone else who had been approached first had simply wanted to go to the party. I'll avoid drawing any conclusion as to which is the more likely explanation.

The phone call galvanised me into action. I changed back into work clothes and made for the car, explaining I didn't know when I'd be back. On the drive to the newsroom I contemplated what lay ahead. There were very few confirmed details, but it had been suggested that a military jet had crashed into a petrol station, and this had started a huge fire. When I got to the office I found mild chaos. Communications out of Lockerbie had been cut, and nothing further had emerged since my phone call. The most important job for me was to get the crew on the road, so I headed for the camera room where they were based. I'd been paired with my crew of choice, and Eric and Allan were bustling around, preparing to put back the equipment they'd removed from their vehicle a couple of hours earlier. The company ran two staff crews and had two of these vans, both liveried Volkswagen Caravelles. However, I knew that the mobile phone in Eric's vehicle wasn't working. It had been a bone of contention for some time, but whoever had responsibility for getting it repaired or replaced had better things to concentrate on. I knew that the ability to communicate would be vital, so I said that we would take the other vehicle. Its phone worked. What's important to understand is that we were in the early days of mobile phones back then. I didn't yet have my own device. That arrived a few weeks later as a reward for what I did that night. The one vehicle phone which worked was hardwired into the dashboard, and the curly lead connecting the handset to its cradle just about reached to my seat in the back if I stretched it hard enough. The attitude towards using it was reminiscent of the experience of one of the other journalists when he first began work at a newspaper in the north-east of England. The office had a single telephone set on its own table, and it was explained to him that, if the need arose for him to use it, he would need to secure permission from the editor first. The use of the vehicles' mobile phones was not quite as restricted, but you were still looked upon with some suspicion if it was discovered that you'd had the temerity to make a call from it. At least that was how it seemed to me.

I was itching to get on the road. But there was one remaining task to be completed before we could leave. Allan, the sound recordist, announced that he was going to fill the flasks, and headed for the canteen. I've teased him about this since, but at the time I was furious at what I saw as a further, unnecessary delay. These flasks were a constant source of friction - not with me, but between the crews and just about everyone else. Each day when we went out to film the world we had little idea of what would face us. The crews would regularly work without a lunch break as we covered developing stories. We'd find ourselves in the middle of nowhere without an opportunity to find food, and the availability of a hot drink and a packet of custard creams made a small but welcome difference. To those who complained about the idea that we were being supplied with free hot water and a biscuit, I usually pointed out that they worked in a dry, heated environment where they could saunter down to the canteen whenever they felt like it to have a tea or coffee and complain about life to their colleagues in some measure of comfort. There was little pleasure to be had from being huddled in a big tin box, trying to keep warm while your anorak and trousers gently steamed from the torrential rain you'd worked in for the last couple of hours, and which was now bouncing off the roof above your head. So the deal was that we were grudgingly given the provisions, and in return we worked hard at showing we were grateful. Allan's assumed role was to keep the supplies in the red plastic box by my seat topped up. Mine was to make the tea, and Eric's was to drink it. He did it well. It's worth acknowledging two other areas of Allan's important ancillary expertise. He had an all-encompassing knowledge of the location of phone boxes and toilets throughout the area that we covered. At times one or other was a veritable life-saver, and was highly valued alongside Eric's similar proficiency in finding fish and chip shops.

Eventually the flasks were filled and we set off through the cars arriving for the Christmas party. Despite knowing that my actions would probably be observed and reported to the appropriate authority, I immediately reached for the phone and dialled the number for RAF Pittreavie, the Search and Rescue Coordination Centre which dealt with aircraft accidents. I read recently that the abilities of our brains have been changed by the arrival of the smart phone. One of the skills which it's made redundant is the need to remember phone numbers. Every number you could ever require can now be stored within an iPhone's capacious memory. Back then, I had to store them in the Mark I brain. I had committed this particular one to memory after an incident following a previous crash involving an RAF fast jet. When I had called directory inquiries, I'd been told that they wouldn't give me the number because it was an Official Secret. Pittreavie's switchboard answered quickly and I asked for the press office. "There are three holding. Do you want to wait?" "Yes."

The crew van joined the M6 motorway, and we began the journey north. I stared out the side window at the lights of the city enveloped in the darkness of a December night. We were at the lowest point of the year, when the days were shortest and the nights longest, and there was a gale buffeting the van from the west. It was going to be an unpleasant evening. I began to worry about how long I'd be on hold. I had learned through bitter experience that the mobile phone network around us was flaky at best, and I knew to make calls at places where I'd have enough time to complete them before coverage disappeared. The last thing I wanted was for the call to be dropped, and for me to have to return to the beginning of the queue when I called back. I also knew that no-one else back in the newsroom would be following this line of enquiry. There wasn't a general understanding of how important a source of information Pittreavie was. As it turned out, my worries over losing the call were groundless. Within a few minutes a voice interrupted my thoughts. "Putting you through." The press officer answered on the first ring. We'd spoken on many occasions in the past, and after we exchanged short pleasantries we quickly got down to business. In the same way that I remember waiting for the 39 bus so many years previously, I know exactly where I was when I heard the news. Just a mile north of Junction 43 of the M6, there's a bridge where the motorway crosses the River Eden. We were there when I heard the press officer say, "It's a Boeing 747." He must have had the same shocked reaction from everyone he'd spoken to that evening, because he waited patiently during the long pause while I absorbed the enormity of what he'd said. I'd been to many crashes before; a

Jaguar fast jet, a Tornado with a crew of two, a Gazelle helicopter, a mid-air collision between two Tornados and another between a Jaguar and a Tornado. But I'd never been to the crash of a 747, and with no major airport within our coverage area, such an incident never seemed possible. I took him through a series of questions, and he answered them quickly and simply. I then left him to move on to the next call, to impart the same information and get the same response. He had a long night ahead.

After I hung up I took a breath and said to the crew, who'd been listening to my end of the conversation but couldn't hear the other end, "It's a 747." A silence descended on the vehicle as they all tried to take in what I'd told them. I quickly dialled the direct line number for the newsroom. It was time to pass on what I'd discovered. One of the copy-takers answered and I said, "I've got copy for you." I heard the paper being wound into the typewriter.

FLASH

A Pan American Airlines Boeing 747 has crashed onto the town of Lockerbie in the South of Scotland. Pan Am Flight 103 was en-route from London Heathrow to John F. Kennedy Airport, New York with 259 people on board when contact was lost. No Mayday call was made before the aircraft disappeared from radar screens at 31,000 feet. A search for survivors has begun. We'll keep you updated on this story throughout the evening, and in our main bulletin after News at Ten.

ENDS

Before long the motorway petered out, and by the time we were approaching the border town of Gretna we were travelling on a two-lane dual carriageway. Ecclefechan, birthplace of writer Thomas Carlyle, drifted by on the left and I began to wonder what I'd encounter ahead. It wasn't long before I found out. I felt the vehicle begin to slow, and glanced up to see why. We were approaching the back of a queue of traffic, about half a mile south of Lockerbie. The crash had closed the road, severing the main west-coast link between Scotland and England, and I suddenly had a new challenge to face. Before I could even begin to cover the story, I had to work out how to get to it. It didn't take me long. I leapt from the vehicle and ran forward down the road, desperately urging the cars and trucks to clear a path for us. Their response wasn't particularly helpful, and I quickly gave up. I trotted back to the crew van and broke the news to the crew. "We're going to have to jog the last bit," I said. I'm not sure what they had expected. Perhaps thoughts had turned to the flasks of hot water, but I urged them out into the cold and wind and they began to pull their equipment from the back. Within a minute we were under way, going much more slowly than I'd have liked, and leaving the electrician, Dave, in the driving seat. We'd got no more than a couple of hundred yards when I glanced back to see if I was going too fast for Eric and Allan. They were a decade older than me, and I tended to forget it at times, oblivious to the toll the passing years took on the body. But as I turned, I saw a sight behind me that raised my spirits. A fire engine from Carlisle was approaching northwards on the southbound carriageway, its flashing blue beacons lighting up the night. Dave had seen it in his mirrors, and had the presence of mind to drive through a gap in the central reservation to follow it. I yelled to the crew, and as Dave arrived alongside us we gratefully jumped back aboard.

The exit for Lockerbie lay just ahead, and we dodged back onto the northbound carriageway to take it, with Dave just managing to squeeze through a gap the fire engine had created in the queue of traffic an instant before the driver of an articulated lorry moved forward to try to block our way. We followed a flyover across the dual carriageway, and within a few seconds were at the entrance to the town. We now faced a new barrier to progress. A group of vigilantes stood in the road ahead, determined to stop rubber-neckers from clogging up the emergency response, and despite our company name emblazoned on the front of the vehicle it was clear they had decided we fell into the category of undesirables. Dave slowed, and I heard a voice shouting "Run them over!" I think it might have been mine. There came a point where the townsfolk and Dave each had to make a decision. Were the people in the road going to move or risk getting run over? And who was the madman in the back seat yelling? Their nerve failed first, and we slid through their ranks to enter the town.

Objective one had been achieved, and we'd arrived in Lockerbie. But what should I do now? To my left behind a row of houses, I could see a fierce fire burning. It seemed as good a place as any to head for. I told Dave to pull over and we decamped once more. I took the team off the main road leading into the town, and entered what I would later understand to be Sherwood Crescent. I had stumbled upon one of the main areas of debris from the aircraft. Less than three hundred yards from here lay the wings and centre section of the Pan Am 747, Maid of the Seas. Within a minute of breaking up high in the skies just south of the town, it occupied an area of space a mile across. Long before the wings, cockpit and engines struck the ground they had lost forward momentum and were travelling vertically. When they hit, the seven fuel tanks, containing sufficient Jet A-1 to carry the aircraft across the Atlantic, erupted into a massive ball of flame so intense that the captain of a British Airways London to Glasgow shuttle overhead Carlisle, twenty-five miles to the south-east, reported it to Scottish Air Traffic Control. It was towards this conflagration that I was leading the crew.

The main Carlisle Road out of Lockerbie, where the crew vehicle was parked, had been quiet when we left it. A few people were walking around, seemingly in a state of shock, but there was little traffic. Sherwood Crescent was like another world. It was eerily deserted, and as we made our way through the darkness I remember wondering where everyone was. It was as if they had shut themselves in their houses in the hope of blotting out the events taking place around them. There was debris on the road, and fires had broken out in some houses. The air was filled with sparks and flying embers, tiny explosions setting off every few seconds as rafters and beams burned. The atmosphere was full of smoke, lending an ethereal quality to the night as the portable light carried by the electrician tried to cut through the haze to illuminate our surroundings for the camera. I moved seemingly in slow motion, my senses at a heightened state of alert, simultaneously looking for shots to direct Eric towards as I also scanned our surroundings for danger. We continued forward, and a fire engine appeared out of the smoke, trying to reverse around cars on the narrow road, its crew having given up the futile fight to bring the huge fuel fire under control. Breathing was becoming more difficult, and we passed a burned-out car, its shell reminiscent of something you would expect to see in a war zone. Eventually I decided we'd gone far enough. The combination of smoke and flames had got to a level where I felt I was endangering our lives. So I stopped, and we turned back towards safety.

A few days later Eric and I would stand looking into this area as we filmed from the A74. The daylight exposed a massive crater where the fire had burned. Beyond it was Sherwood Crescent, its tarmac coming to a sudden end on the crater's edge, like a cliff-side road which had collapsed into the sea. A vast area of land had been vapourised by the intense heat. Just beyond the now precipitous end of Sherwood Crescent I saw the burned out car I'd passed on the fateful night. In a curious way it was like seeing a familiar friend, someone I'd shared a moment with during a time of great stress. But then I noticed it was only a few short yards from where the road disappeared. There came the dawning realisation of just how close we'd come to the crater's edge in the dark and the smoke as we sought to bring the story to the world.

Emerging from the darkness of Sherwood Crescent, I began to balance the pictures I now had with available time. My target was to get our coverage on News at Ten, and I'd have to be leaving soon to achieve it. The images we'd got from Sherwood Crescent were dramatic, and now I needed some human reaction to qualify them. I approached a woman standing in her open doorway watching the scene before her, and soon she was telling her tale for the camera. She told me of the bang as the aircraft hit the ground, followed by a whoosh as the fireball erupted. It was vivid in her mind, and I could see her reliving the experience as she spoke. We wandered a little way down the road towards the town centre as I looked for something else to complete my report. It wasn't long before it arrived. I turned to look behind me and saw three ambulances approaching at speed, blue beacons flashing and sirens wailing their baleful cry. "Turn over!" I called to Eric, and he was instantly aware there was something urgent to film. No other cameraman I worked with had his ease of operation in such highly charged situations, and I was grateful to have him with me that night. As I was, equally, for the presence of Allan and Dave.

An alarm clock was now ringing in my head. I had all of the components I required, but I still needed to get them to ITN, ITV's news provider, for News at Ten. And to do that, the tape we'd shot would have to be taken physically back to Carlisle. I decided to split the crew. Eric, Allan and Dave would stay in Lockerbie while I would take the tape back, since I didn't know if I'd have to edit a report, or whether ITN would handle that aspect themselves. We made our way back to the crew van, but before we reached it there was an incident which could have had a serious impact on our work. I'd been concerned following our contact with the vigilantes on our way into Lockerbie. It had highlighted another aspect of the perilous situation we'd been about to enter. Not only were we putting ourselves in danger from the smoke and the fire, we were also being exposed to a situation where some members of the civil population had decided to take the law into their own hands. Their quite understandable desire to protect the town from outsiders could easily escalate rapidly, given the shock and emotion of the moment. At such a time it was vital that we not present ourselves as targets. But sometimes events have a way of circumventing resolve.

As we hurried along I was issuing instructions to the crew, explaining my plan of action in the knowledge that Eric was more than capable of continuing to cover events without my presence. As we passed an articulated lorry which had parked up to escape the chaos, its driver spotted the camera, and offered the benefit of his views on what we were doing there. It was obvious that he was upset by what was happening around him, and it's often human nature to lash out when the world becomes difficult to understand. Eric responded sharply, and there was an immediate flash of tempers. If he'd read *The Art of War* during his long, lonely nights in the cab, the driver would have realised that, being outnumbered four to one, beginning a fight was not the wisest thing to do. But it seemed that was what was about to occur. I stepped in quickly to calm the situation, fearful that a physical altercation could set back my attempts to reach Carlisle with the tape, and potentially injure Eric enough to stop him from further filming. I apologised to the driver, and told him I understood his viewpoint. But we, like him, had a job to do. The tension was broken, and I took the opportunity to push Eric gently away. Both parties seemed secretly relieved that the moment had passed without anyone feeling they'd lost face.

We arrived back at the van and the crew began to pull out extra batteries to sustain their operations until they could be re-supplied. Eric ejected from the camera the tape he'd shot and gave it to me, secure in its protective box. I grabbed the keys from Dave and jumped into the front seat. The engine roared into life. As soon as I heard the back door slam shut I executed a rather wild three-point turn which succeeded in scattering the pedestrians who were passing by, and then I was off, reaching the A74 south in a matter of seconds for the journey back. In the rush to get away the flasks of hot water had been forgotten. Having made the journey northwards to Lockerbie, they were now travelling at speed back in the direction of Carlisle.

The northbound carriageway was still at a standstill, the end of the tailback of vehicles having extended much further southwards in the time since we'd arrived. However, my side of the road was deserted, its traffic halted in a similar queue to the north of the town. The A74 had not been built to motorway standards. and I took to using the full width of both lanes to reduce the radius of bends, and with it the risk of anything going awry. We'd chosen this vehicle because the phone in Eric's didn't work, but we'd no idea how bad its handling was. Of course the westerly gale didn't help, pushing hard against the van's slab side, but it was obvious something was seriously wrong. It drove like the shock absorbers had been disconnected, leaving the body to float and bounce about precariously on its uncontained springs. On every bend I was convinced it was about to topple over.

As I sped south I punched the redial button on the phone. The device had an external speaker, and if you didn't remove the handset from its holder you could hear the other end of the conversation through it. Unfortunately the van was so noisy, and the external microphone so useless, that any attempt at a two-way conversation was difficult at best. My call was answered by Carol, and I began shouting at the top of my voice in the hope that she'd hear me above the background noise. "I'm on my way back," I yelled. "I may be with you in twenty minutes."

I pressed on and eventually the lights of Carlisle came into sight. I felt as though I had crossed a divide. Everything ahead appeared normal, yet behind me a disaster of immense proportions was unfolding, with huge resources on the way to the scene for the rescue and recovery work. As I arrived into the car park, for the second time that night I scattered a few pedestrians out of the way. My observations about the apparent normality of life here were confirmed as I realised the pedestrians were, if I can put it delicately, with drink. It was with astonishment that I saw the staff Christmas party was still in full swing. It was the first of a number of revelations around the Lockerbie crash that created a watershed in my opinions. But if I felt any anger or resentment at their lack of compassion for those who had surely lost their lives, there was no time to express it. I burst through the door into reception to be met by Carol. She told me they were waiting for the tape in telecine, the technical area which would send our footage to London. As I ran down the corridor, I pulled the tape from its box and gave it to a technician. "It needs rewound," I explained. He pushed it into the slot on the face of a video recorder and pressed the rewind button. Within a few seconds the tape came to a halt at the beginning, and he pressed play. It was then that an extraordinary transformation took place as my brain caught up with my body. The pictures we'd shot came to life on the screens around the room. Despite my having been there less than half an hour before, seeing, smelling and tasting the fire and destruction, it all seemed curiously new, as though it was somewhere else. In London and around the world video recorders captured the events I'd witnessed, before replaying them to shocked audiences. The room was silent as we looked on. The clock on the wall marked the time. Five minutes to ten.

I left and made my way upstairs to the newsroom. It was a bustle of activity, but most eyes turned towards me when I entered. I couldn't quite identify it, but there was something in their eyes that I felt I should recognise. It was as if they were looking at me differently. And of course they would have been justified in doing so. The last couple of hours had changed me. I was a different person from the one who had left the building earlier, as were Eric, Allan and Dave. But could it be so plainly written on my face? As I saw News at Ten start on a screen in the corner, someone told me that ITN wanted to interview me. I have to say at this point that they were superb that night. I knew how long they'd had my pictures, and yet here they were just a few seconds later, opening the programme. There was the shot of the three ambulances racing into town; pictures of the houses in Sherwood Crescent on fire; and the woman who had so eloquently described what she'd heard and seen. If I was proud of what I'd achieved so far that evening, I was equally proud of what ITN managed to do in such a short space of time. I was gently brought back from my thoughts as a voice reminded me about the interview. But I recognised there was a problem. A short while previously we'd had a new telephone system installed, and with it came new desk phones. They were awful. Certainly, I no longer had to force a rotary dial around to make a phone call. Now I simply pushed a few buttons and was connected as if by magic. But the earpieces were so quiet that I could barely make out what was being said at the other end, and despite complaining vehemently about the fault since installation, nothing had been done to improve matters. If I did the interview from the newsroom, the voice of Alastair Stewart in the London studio would be nothing more than a faint mumble beneath the background noise. So I asked for the call to be transferred to a side office and shut myself in there. I spent a minute or two telling my version of events live on air, before emerging once more into the newsroom. And there it was again. That look in their eyes. It was beginning to annoy me.

We took no pleasure that night from the fact that we had roundly beaten the BBC to get the first pictures on air. It didn't seem right to indulge in petty rivalries at such a significant moment.

The night passed in a bit of a blur. I did more interviews with television stations around the world on the phone, and on camera. It was while I was removing the make-up someone else had applied for me that I saw something odd. Beneath the powder which flattened reflections for the camera, my skin was filthy. I was puzzled for a moment as I tried to work out what it was. And then I remembered the smoke and the flames. My face was carrying unmistakable evidence of where I had been. I was wearing the fallout from the crater containing the centre section of Pan Am 103.

I was weary by the time I got to bed after 6 am, but sleep evaded me. The horrific images from the night before were playing in my head as if on the endless loop of some internal video tape recorder. At seven the phone rang and destroyed any chance of rest. It was a journalist I knew from Manx Radio who'd heard one of the reports I'd done and wanted an interview for their morning news programme. Afterwards, I gave up the idea of sleep and showered, washing away the remaining detritus from the fire. But although the hot water cleansed my body, it could do little to wipe away the memories in my head. I ate breakfast in silence, and eventually made my way back to the office to catch up on developments.

As the morning wore on it was decided that our evening news programme would come live from Lockerbie that night, and I was to be involved in anchoring it. The outside broadcast unit was duly dispatched, sent to find a suitable location for the transmission. I arrived on site about midday to find a surprising air of calm. One of the editors was hunched in a makeshift edit suite set up in the back of a people carrier. He worked tirelessly to put together story after story, including some for overseas broadcasters who made use of our facilities. One of the most remarkable of these reports was by a seasoned American reporter, a veteran of covering the Vietnam War. His was a style I'd never witnessed before, and it was both authoritative and moving. In some ways it mirrored the approach of Alistair Cooke on his radio series, Letter From America. But instead of the authentic English accent, a Texan drawl issued from beneath a large cowboy hat. His personality was powerful, with a mastery of language and storytelling to be envied. He spoke to camera of an incident he'd witnessed on one of Lockerbie's estates as he and his cameraman watched a council worker go about his job. This man's task was to retrieve a body, still strapped in an aircraft seat, from the roof of a house. Someone else had already climbed up to provide a measure of dignity by covering the body with a tarpaulin. The worker placed his ladder against the side of the house and carefully ascended, taking with him a second ladder to allow him to reach the chimney across the slates. Having secured it in place, he climbed back down for a rope to tie around the seat. Slowly, as if trying to delay the moment for as long as possible, he climbed up the first ladder and transferred to the second, before eventually reaching the ridge tiles. With delicate care he passed the rope around the chimney and finally tied its end to the seat. There followed a pause in proceedings, almost as if he were steeling himself for the next part, the lowering of the seat and its occupant safely to the ground. The previous day this worker may have been repairing a bathroom, sweeping a street, or carrying out any of the myriad mundane daily tasks a council is expected to fulfill. But today he was retrieving a body which had fallen from the sky in the night, and he was struggling to understand how his life had been touched in this way. On the pavement below someone walked by, lost in their own thoughts, oblivious of the scene above. On the roof, the man began to move, as if preparing for the final phase of the operation. But he paused again, indulging in some internal debate with his conscience. At length he arrived at a decision and, with a tender respect for the person this once had been, moved the tarpaulin just enough to see the face. His curiosity satisfied in a heartbeat, he replaced it gently and turned his head away. Only he would know whether the final expression was one of pain or peace, but it was an image which would likely stay with him for the rest of his life.

All of these details were presented in a carefully measured report with the pictures of the poignant scene overlaid in editing. The gnarled Texan's pay-off was one which has as great an impact on me today as it had back then. Looking straight at the lens, he said, "There are days when you'd rather not have been where you've been or seen what you've seen. Today was one of those days." Few in Lockerbie could disagree.

That evening's programme was not an easy one to present. Each one of us there had an emotional investment in the story, and the pressures on us to get the tone right were enormous. But as we came off air I felt that everyone had done a good job. I think it was at this point that I learned I had been chosen to present the late night bulletin, which that night was scheduled for midnight. We worked throughout the evening on its content, and it was decided that I would interview another American reporter live on air. As we approached twelve o'clock I could feel my energy levels draining rapidly. By now I had been awake and working for nearly forty hours, and my brain had decided enough was enough. I needed one last rush of adrenaline to make it through the bulletin, and then I could head home to sleep. I took my place with a few minutes to spare. It was nearly midnight, the night was cold and black, and I was being blinded by the lights illuminating me for the camera. They made it almost impossible to read my script or notes, and difficult to pick out the red tally light above the lens that showed me where in the glare I needed to look. I was joined by the American reporter, and over the course of the next few minutes I must have asked him his name more than half a dozen times. I have trouble with names at the best of times, but here, on the verge of exhaustion, I had no hope. Whether he could see how desperately tired I was, I'll never know. But he was very polite and patient, repeating his name at each of my requests with no hint of annoyance. Far too quickly I heard the production assistant's voice in my earpiece counting me into the bulletin. She reached zero and I was live. Somehow I managed to read the words on the bits of paper in my hand, the script relating events of the time since the Maid of the Seas had crashed. It all seemed to be going well. But then I reached the interview. As I began to introduce my guest I heard my voice approach the point where I needed his name. And I knew I didn't know it. There was a frantic scramble in my head as, having given up any hope of conjuring it out of a befuddled brain, I searched for an alternative way of introducing him into the bulletin. This thought process took place in a second or two at most, but then the moment was upon me. I took a courageous and brave stab in the dark and came out with an effort that sounded very close to Bumovitz. I'm quite sure there is no-one in this world with the family name Bumovitz. But I reasoned that, if I said it confidently enough, I might just get away with it. I saw a brief flare of anger in the man's eyes, but then his professionalism kicked in, and he began to answer my question. We continued the conversation for perhaps two minutes, before I wrapped up and began to read the closing headlines. By the time I came off air, my American friend had slipped off into the night and any chance of apologising was lost forever.

Christmas came and went. It wasn't a joyous affair, but however I felt, it was nothing compared with what the people of Lockerbie were going through. Working alongside them were the tireless responders - police and other emergency services, mountain rescue teams, forensic teams, air accident investigators, council employees and many more - who were dealing with a crime scene, whilst trying to restore some semblance of normality to a distraught community. Meanwhile, the incident had been confirmed as having been caused by a bomb. I returned to Lockerbie with Eric and Allan to make a programme about events, scheduled to transmit that Friday night. In making it, I found the answer to something which had been puzzling me. Initial reports had suggested an aircraft had flown into a petrol station, and I was interested to discover how that had come about. The riddle was solved when I stopped to chat with a police traffic officer. It turned out that he was from Strathclyde Police, the next force to the north of Lockerbie. The town itself lies within Dumfries and Galloway, and the local officers who knew the area like the back of their hand were a part of Dumfries and Galloway Constabulary. Today, all of the discrete police forces north of the border have been combined into one unit, Police Scotland. When the Maid of the Seas crashed it severed communications with the town. Whether for that reason, or as a response to the report of a huge fire from the British Airways shuttle captain, this traffic officer was sent south to investigate what was happening. When he arrived in unfamiliar surroundings to find the biggest blaze he had likely ever seen, it was not unreasonable to conclude that it must be a fuel fire, and that the only possible source of the fuel was a petrol station.

Dumfries and Galloway was a small police force, and they were in danger of being overwhelmed by the event. Help was brought in from Strathclyde amongst others to fill a number of roles. One of them was press officer. He was very good at what he did, but we clashed from the beginning. As with the traffic officer, he was in unfamiliar territory, only he didn't seem to know it. Lockerbie was very firmly our territory, but in most dealings it seemed to me that he gave preference to our neighbours from the north, STV. I'm sure it wasn't a deliberate snub. Maybe it was unfair to expect him to know the intimate details of where the service areas of the various television stations began and ended, but because he was normally based in Glasgow he knew the STV journalists, and I was left out, relatively speaking, in the cold. It was a situation that would never end well.

Its conclusion came in a vignette that caused us a lot of amusement, and him a little discomfort. I stood with Eric in the car park of Lockerbie Academy awaiting the arrival of Prime Minister Margaret Thatcher. She was coming to pay her respects to the 270 people who had died, and to show the government's support for the town. The press officer was with me, and I was trying hard to form some sort of relationship which might bridge the chasm I felt existed. He'd already seen me in conversation with the constituency MP Hector Monro, and I could see him beginning to reassess me. The turning point came a few minutes later when Dumfries and Galloway's Chief Constable passed by. He glanced across and spotted me amongst the crowd before shouting, "Ian! Nice to see you. Border Television! My favourite TV station!" I laughed, and shouted some appropriate response of thanks. The brief encounter threw a switch in the press officer's mind. He reasoned that if I was the Chief Constable's favourite I'd better be his too. From that point forward we got on much better.

It had been a few days since I'd seen Eric. Although we'd spoken on the phone to catch up, neither of us had worked on Christmas Day or Boxing Day. He told me of one incident after I'd left him on the night of the crash, and of how it had come back to haunt him a couple of days later. After my hurried departure with the pictures, he'd walked down the road towards the town centre and discovered one of the aircraft's engines embedded, still smoking, in the tarmac. He had begun filming it, walking around the massive piece of machinery, when Allan suddenly grabbed him roughly. It was understood we never touched a cameraman whilst filming because it would likely unbalance him and ruin the shot. But on this occasion Allan had good reason. As Eric shot him a quizzical look, he pointed to the ground. To his horror, Eric saw that he'd been about to step on the body of a young woman. She was instantly memorable because of her long, crimped blonde hair. The following Saturday morning, Christmas Eve, he was at home when he heard the newspaper drop onto the mat at the door. He went to collect it and froze in shock as he picked it up. Staring back at him from the front page of the Daily Mail was a photograph of the same girl.

We drove out of Lockerbie, travelling east on the road towards Langholm. It quickly climbed two hundred feet to Tundergarth. Across the narrow country B-road from the church there's farmland, and in an otherwise unremarkable pasture lay the cockpit of the Maid of the Seas. Despite its six mile fall from the sky it was largely intact. The image became the icon of Lockerbie for me, and as I stood there I tried not to think of the final few minutes of those who had been inside as they plunged to the ground. It was a chastening moment. Before then I had seen wreckage of individual small parts of the aircraft, but this was its brain, the place where decisions had been made and instructions issued to control the leviathan behind. It was a forlorn image to see it at rest more than two miles away from where the wings and centre section had landed.

One other place remains etched in my mind above most. A makeshift mortuary had been set up in the Town Hall, a few yards away from Lockerbie's War Memorial. As the bodies were recovered from their various resting places they were brought here for identification. On the pavement outside, there was a growing collection of flowers, placed or sent there by those who wanted to pay their respects to the dead. Amongst them was one bouquet which brought a tear to my eye. Pan Am 103 had begun its journey in Frankfurt. The flight was sold as a single through ticket to New York, but during a stop at Heathrow passengers were required to change aircraft. These flowers had been sent by a couple who had travelled only on the Frankfurt to London sector, disembarking from the aircraft before its passengers continued on their fateful journey. While on board, they had made friends with a young girl who had died within a short time of them saying goodbye. The card attached to the blooms read simply, *To the Little Girl in the Red Dress.*

By Thursday I had relocated to an edit suite to begin the work of constructing the programme for the following night. We would normally allocate a week for the task, so completing it in two days would be a difficult. I had access, not only to the material I had shot with Eric on the night and in the days since then, but also to the pictures shot by the other cameramen who'd been there. The editor and I closed the door and got down to work.

I enjoy filming, but editing is where the hard work that's put into a programme finally comes together and the production takes on an identifiable shape. I would later be responsible for bringing non-linear editing to the company, but at this point we used a linear editing system, which involved copying pictures from one tape to another. It was a step-change from the days of film production, when the editor made physical cuts to the medium and joined the shots together with sticky tape. It may seem antiquated now, but back then it was the only technology we had. The move to non-destructive linear editing meant we didn't destroy what we'd shot when we came to edit it. But its linear nature meant there was little chance to go back and change things once decisions had been made, and this provided an added pressure. I liken today's non-linear editing on computers to writing a novel on a word processor. If you want to go back to the beginning of the book and change a paragraph, it's a simple enough task. But linear editing offers no such opportunity. It's like using a typewriter to write the novel. If you want to take out a paragraph on page one, you need to re-type everything from there to the end. From my point of view it meant that I had to get the construction of the programme right first time.

We ploughed on through Thursday, making good progress as I reviewed the available pictures and worked hard to create a logical storyline. By the time the building began to empty I was comfortable with where we were. But I also knew we wouldn't be able to make the sort of progress which would allow us to go home any time soon. As we pressed on into the evening the frustrations I would regularly feel when I worked abnormal hours began to grow. The vast majority of people who worked around me did a nine-to-five job. The organisation was designed to cater - quite literally - for this group of employees. You could get tea, coffee and a bacon roll in the morning, a good lunch shortly after midday, and a cup of tea and a chocolate biscuit during the afternoon. But if your work extended into the evening you were on your own. There was a fish and chip shop a couple of hundred yards away, and an excellent Chinese take-away three-quarters of a mile down the road, but going there involved disconnecting from the production, and it always took time afterwards to regain the thought processes which had been in my head. I spent years arguing just to get a cold drinks machine installed, but then I'd sometimes find that it hadn't been filled before everyone else went home. That raised my blood pressure too. In the end I managed to find a partial solution to hunger. I would go on what became known as my Sausage Hunt. I had discovered that the left-over sausages from breakfast were stored in the refrigerator overnight, to be re-heated and served the following day. I reasoned that I was actually doing everyone else a good turn by tracking down these escapees and removing them from circulation. Cold sausages may not be a gourmet's dream, but when you're desperate for food and cross with the world I can assure you they go down a treat. I had occasionally thought of firing up the kitchen cookers to make a meal, but I didn't think I'd get away with that. Just how successful that night's Sausage Hunt was I don't recall.

I'm not sure that I made any formal decision to work through the night. It just sort of happened. And the longer the editor and I continued, the more our efficiency level dropped. By 5 am there were moments when we were both hallucinating. The room had not been designed for creativity. There was a cold, clinical feel about it, the bare white walls reflecting the unforgiving glare from fluorescent tubes on the ceiling. The noise from the video tape machines seemed to increase in volume as we got tired, and began to beat on our eardrums. At one point the editor and I fell asleep at the same time. Along with the noise and the harsh light, I swear the walls began to move. We ached for release from this prison cell, but the ever-present spectre of passing time kept us at work. At 6 am the cleaners arrived, and we welcomed other human presence, opening the door so we could hear them as they chatted. By 9 am the office workers had made it in, looking healthily fresh and prepared for the day ahead. In comparison, we were dishevelled, unkempt and unshaven, bleary-eyed, and frankly, slightly smelly. But we worked on, our brains constantly calculating remaining work against available time. Finally, at some point late that afternoon I was done. My brain could relax a little, though not too much in case I fell asleep again. The editor, meanwhile, had the task of putting the programme to bed, to make it ready for transmission. My boss came to view our work. She cried. I felt it was as fitting a reaction to the programme as I could think of.

Tucked away in the corner of Sherwood Crescent where the road doubles back on itself, close to the spot where the fire consumed all around, there's now a simple garden of remembrance. Occasionally if I'm passing I'll follow the route I walked all those years ago to stand there for a few minutes in contemplation. New bungalows have been built nearby, distinct from the design of the houses elsewhere on the road, a small clue to the destruction which befell this place in 1988. I returned not long ago, filming for an ITV programme which revisited the tragedy. I noticed a woman arrive and park on one of the driveways, and I walked across to speak to her, much to the horror of the producer who was working with me, who felt I'd be intruding. But this place felt familiar. I had connections with it which could only have been created in adversity, and felt a kinship with its people. I introduced myself and there was a flicker of recognition. I asked about her cat, a friendly marmalade creature who'd greeted me like a long lost friend on one of my visits. She told me with sadness how she'd lost her the previous year. As the cameraman and producer looked on, surprised at the ease of our conversation, I told her about my experiences on the night of the crash, and of the car I'd walked past when I came close to falling into the crater. I pointed to where it had been, and her response was unexpected. "It was my car," she said.

That same day I drove up the hill, retracing my steps to Tundergarth, and stopped again in the car park of the church. A small gate across the driveway opens into the churchyard, and I walked around the stone-built church to a smaller building, tastefully designed to match its larger neighbour. Inside lie two books. One is a visitors book signed by those who have come, each for their own reason, to the place where the icon of the Lockerbie Disaster landed. The other is a carefully gathered collection of information in tribute to the life of each person who died that night. It's difficult to define my emotions during visits to either of these two spots. Each of them changed my own life, and the way that I observe the lives of others. The man who left the newsroom in a search for a plane crash came back a very different person. Perhaps that was really the transformation people saw which caused them to look at me so strangely that night.

There's a connection with Lockerbie that I stumbled upon a quarter of a century afterwards. Whilst working on another project I had persuaded the former government Minister Michael Portillo to take part in an interview. I collected him from the railway station in Lancaster and took him to the venue he was appearing at that evening in Morecambe. He was an affable and likeable interviewee, and afterwards Eric and I chatted with him about a range of subjects. Our presence as the first television crew at Lockerbie came up, and he smiled as I explained how our pictures led News at Ten that night and told him of the circumstances of my interview immediately afterwards on the less than perfect phone. He spoke about his own recollection of the same few minutes. There had been a number of votes scheduled in the Commons that evening, and Members were passing through the lobby on a regular basis. He was in the company of then Prime Minister Margaret Thatcher discussing events, and each time their vote had been registered, he explained that they would rush back to a television set to catch up with what was happening on News at Ten.

My programme having been made and transmitted, I turned my attention back to other productions. In early January Eric and I stood at a window in Manchester Airport. We had wandered a few yards away from the departure gate to look at the aircraft which was about to fly us across the Atlantic. I was taking a retired miner from West Cumbria and the former Mayor of the town of Whitehaven on a mission to explore the historical connections between their area and the eastern seaboard of the United States. The huge British Airways Boeing 747 stood ready for us to board. As we gazed at it our thoughts returned to Lockerbie, to the field across the road from Tundergarth church where the cockpit of the Maid of the Seas had lain. The image was clear in our minds as the most tangible memory of a night we'd never forget. It was an emotional moment. Very quietly, in a voice only just audible above the hubbub around us I said, "It seems so strange to see the cockpit still in place." We steeled ourselves, and turned back to the gate to begin boarding.

There were two outcomes from my programme, both within weeks of each other. It was shortlisted for an award at The Royal Television Society's annual bash in the region. I'm told there was an almighty row between the judges over the jury's decision, but my supporters on it lost out. The jury decided that the events of Lockerbie afforded less of an impact on the area than the career of a footballer, and the award went instead to a programme about him. I wasn't overly upset about it, though I did think it was an odd decision. However, shortly afterwards I received news that I had been more successful with another jury. This wasn't a collection of regional programme makers. Instead, I discovered I was to be honoured by the prestigious New York Film and Television Festival. I looked upon it as a vindication of my work. But in an odd twist of fate another rebuff awaited me. This time it would come, not from the award jury, but from my own company. In a decision I wasn't a part of, it was determined that someone else would travel to New York to collect the award on my behalf. Not only had this person not had anything to do with my programme, as far as I was aware they had never set foot in Lockerbie. Someone once said, "Don't let them fool you by saying that success breeds success. Success merely breeds envy, and for some, opportunity." So the opportunity was grabbed, and I eventually collected my medal, not on the stage of an internationally renowned media festival, but in a slightly seedy back office next to the management lavatory. Michelle Obama said, "When they go low, we go high." I simply smiled and shook the hand of my presenter. If my own importance in creating this award-winning programme was an inconvenience, I was happy to acknowledge the part played by Eric, Allan and Dave in making such a success of the job we did that night, and I made sure they each received a duplicate of my medal, paid for out of my own pocket. Over the quarter-century since, I have been surprised on a regular basis to discover claims made by former colleagues about the role they played at Lockerbie, and I was determined to pre-empt a land-grab of involvement-by-association by providing my crew with a memento of the respect I had for their professionalism and bravery.

The stories of Susan Maxwell and Lockerbie are the most extreme examples of the challenges which faced me over the years. Each day was a new adventure, and for the most part they were filled with laughter as I approached the task in hand with humour and a resilience which often surprised those around me. I have a strong bond with those who worked closely with me, particularly the film crew members I trusted to help me battle the inconsistencies of an often intransigent world. Without their devotion this book would be emptier and far less colourful.

I've been fortunate to reach a position where I could follow my instincts and drive progress in the direction I believed to be right. The approach is best summed up by the words of the American writer Ralph Waldo Emmerson, and I would commend it as an epithet for an enjoyable and successful career.

Do not go where the path may lead. Go instead where there is no path, and leave a trail.

INDEX

9 781999 813703